Business Networking

A Scientific Method

D. Scott Smith, MBA

Business Networking

D. Scott Smith, MBA

Business Networking

D. Scott Smith, MBA

ISBN: 979-8-8692-5480-1

For information email
scott@dscottsmith.com

Learn more at dscottsmith.com

Business Networking

D. Scott Smith, MBA

Table Of Contents

Preface

The inception of this comprehensive guide on Business Networking can be traced back to a personal pledge I made in 2012. Over the years, I have been privileged to be in the company of numerous extraordinary individuals, including family members, friends, colleagues, and clients. Each one of these people held a wealth of knowledge, expertise, and skill within them. Time and time again, I would find myself in awe of their innate ability to enhance the lives of those around them through the application of their talents.

None of these individuals was born with such knowledge or skills; instead, they nurtured and honed them over time. While perusing a widely-read article on the science of learning and knowledge retention, it dawned on me that many of us tend to undervalue the significance of our own abilities and how they can be of immense benefit to others. As a result, I made a commitment for 2012 to consciously remind people of their own remarkable qualities and potential.

In 2016, I delivered a talk at the Social Media Summit in Dublin, Ireland, titled "The Psychology and Physiology of Relationships." My presentation delved into the academic research that underscored the importance and value of cultivating relationships. I highlighted that by forging relationships, we create a sense of responsibility toward the other person. I coined the phrase "Engage and Validate" to encapsulate this obligation. By connecting (engaging) with others, we should validate them through attentive listening. I encouraged the audience to become "Motivational Listeners."

As I delved deeper into the subject, I eventually distilled the principles of being a Motivational Listener. From there, I designed a course to impart this knowledge to others. I have had the good fortune to be invited to speak at various events on this subject and have often been asked about the availability of a book covering the topic. It is truly humbling to realize that the insights I have gathered are deemed valuable enough to be compiled into a book.

If I were to embark on writing such a book, it was imperative for it to possess practical applications. Motivational Listeners can have a profound impact on lives in myriad ways, and one aspect particularly close to my heart is their potential to act as connectors, building robust human networks. In this book, I present the scientific foundation supporting the process of business networking, as I believe it is crucial to understand the underlying mechanisms at play.

It is an immense honor to know that you are taking the time to read these words. I trust that you will derive value from the practical steps I have outlined for achieving success at networking events. Who knows? Maybe one day, our paths will cross, and we will have the opportunity to meet in person – after all, the future is full of surprises.

Overview

I am pragmatic. My interest in the actions we take. Bumper sticker platitudes leave me empty. I have added a handful of these at the end of this section – just for reference. See how many of them you have heard.

Let me take one for an example, "Live life to the fullest." Since there are over eight billion people on the planet then there are as many ways to accomplish such a goal. This may mean abandoning responsibility and living a life of indulgence. It may be focusing on only the important aspects of life. What I am looking for is a set of instructions, actions, positive steps which move me in a forward direction.

When it comes to business networking we often hear, "your network is your net worth" (Tim Sanders). This is interesting but does not tell me how to build my network. In this book I combine two of my previous works to provide a manual on networking.

In the first part of this book we examine the brain science around how we connect. Then I give you a formula, a process to connect at networking events. These events can be in-person or virtual – the method will work in both situations. I believe we need to understand the mechanics of a process and not simply memorizing a networking script..

The problem with scripts is that the use will run into trouble following the script when the conversation does not go as planned. Since networking is all about human-to-human connection, the engagement will never follow a prescribed plan.

When we have an understanding of the fundamentals and the plan changes, we can adapt. That is what humans do well – adapt. The brain science provides a basis for taking the method I give and allow you to adapt it to your personality and style.

The second part of this book focuses on a practical method and process to build your network. You might well ask me why I did not put this as the first part of book. Consider this book as a technical manual. In such a book you turn to the section you need when you want a specific answer. Since I wrote the part about networking at events first, I put it at the front of this book. Feel free to jump to the second half and look at the framework of an effective business network.

Keep this book close-by when you attend your next event. Review the steps to connect with individuals that are alone or in groups. How to "test the waters" and see if they are interested in a conversation. Or jump to the back and look at your business network structure – find the gaps and develop a plan to fill your network with the right people.

I have worked with introverts, extroverts, ambiverts, and those all along the continuum. There is no magic type of personality that is a better or worse networker. This is a skill which you can learn, master, and use as an effective business tool.

Motivational Quotes:

"Believe you can and you're halfway there." – Theodore Roosevelt

"The only limit to our realization of tomorrow will be our doubts of today." – Franklin D. Roosevelt

"The journey of a thousand miles begins with a single step." – Lao Tzu

"Don't count the days, make the days count." – Muhammad Ali

"Only those who dare to fail greatly can ever achieve greatly." – Robert F. Kennedy

"Live life to the fullest."

"You miss 100% of the shots you don't take." – Wayne Gretzky

"It's not whether you get knocked down, it's whether you get up." – Vince Lombardi

"The future belongs to those who believe in the beauty of their dreams." – Eleanor Roosevelt

"Never, never, never give up." – Winston Churchill

"No one can make you feel inferior without your consent." – Eleanor Roosevelt

"I can and I will."

"Do or do not, there is no try." – Yoda, Star Wars

"Success is not final, failure is not fatal: It is the courage to continue that counts." – Winston Churchill

"Life is a journey, not a destination."

"If you can dream it, you can do it." – Walt Disney

"Dream big and dare to fail." – Norman Vaughan

"The only way to do great work is to love what you do." – Steve Jobs

"Don't stop until you're proud."

"Turn your wounds into wisdom." – Oprah Winfrey

"You are stronger than you think."

"Make today amazing."

"Be the change you wish to see in the world." – Mahatma Gandhi

"Pain is temporary, quitting lasts forever." – Lance Armstrong

"What would you do if you were not afraid?"

"Always stay humble and kind."

"You are enough just as you are."

"Every day may not be good, but there's something good in every day."

"Embrace the detours."

"Be fearless in the pursuit of what sets your soul on fire."

Introduction to Becoming a Motivational Listener

Motivational Listening is a powerful approach aimed at ensuring that the speaker leaves a conversation feeling more positive about themselves than when they entered. Leveraging the insights offered by neuroscience, Motivational Listening is a structured process designed to foster connections with others, even in unfamiliar situations like trade shows or conventions. This technique enables you to rapidly build rapport with people you have never met before.

In any organization, attending networking events is often a necessity, whether by choice or as a job requirement. However, not everyone is naturally at ease in such environments. Success in networking is not exclusive to extroverts and is not be hindered by introversion. The objective is to optimize your time at these events, create authentic connections, and leave a lasting impression as an engaging individual.

The primary aim of this book is to impart a specific technique for meeting and getting to know new people at networking events. By providing practical tools and step-by-step guidance, this book equips you to become a master networker and, ultimately, a Motivational Listener.

Business Networking

Drawing on the science and research of physiology and psychology, Motivational Listening delves into the intricacies of human relationships. Our brains, which consume more energy than any other organ in our body, are incredibly complex and powerful. To put it in perspective, if a state-of-the-art supercomputer attempted to process the amount of information our brains handle in just one second, it would take 40 minutes to do so!

As mentioned earlier, Motivational Listening is a purposeful process designed to uplift the speaker, rather than manipulate or insincerely flatter them. The aim is to cultivate genuine relationships that enrich both your professional and personal life.

Motivational Listening can be employed by business owners and managers to develop employees and remind them of their value. When employees learn this skill, they can enhance and strengthen customer relations. The primary focus of this book, however, is to enable individuals to quickly establish rapport with new acquaintances at networking events.

Some may wonder if Motivational Listening is synonymous with Active Listening. While Active Listening is indeed a technique for engaging with a speaker, it lacks the directed process for rapport-building that is inherent in Motivational Listening. However, Active Listening skills, such as paying attention, minimizing distractions, and monitoring body language and audible cues, are incorporated into the Motivational Listening approach. We will explore the nuances of Active Listening in more detail later in the book.

As a Motivational Listener, you recognize the speaker's uniqueness and guide them towards realizing that their knowledge and skills are anything but commonplace. I will delve deeper into this aspect later on.

In this book, I will provide the rationale for becoming a Motivational Listener. I trust that you will be able to utilize these skills to expand your network, advance your career, and grow your business. On a more profound level, you may offer encouragement to someone who truly needs it. When you attend networking events as a Motivational Listener, you will be perceived as fascinating, primarily because you are genuinely interested in others.

Networking: Understanding the Essence and Debunking Myths

Let us delve into the true essence of networking and dispel the misconceptions surrounding it. Let's begin by addressing what networking should never be: advertising. Advertising is the act of conveying a succinct message about your product or service to a vast audience, who may have a problem that you can solve, thereby turning them into potential customers.

Networking at events should not involve attempting to distribute your message or business card to every attendee. There are stories of "hit and run" networkers – individuals who hurriedly circulate the room, thrusting a business card into everyone's hand. This approach is not only ineffective but also comes across as impolite. Surprisingly, such practices persist even in contemporary times.

I recently witnessed this phenomenon at a networking event. As I sat at a table, getting acquainted with a new person, we fell victim to a "hit and run" networker. The individual hurriedly tossed a pair of his business cards between us, muttered something incoherent, and continued on his way. Baffled, my conversation partner and I exchanged puzzled glances and left the cards untouched on the table.

Business Networking

Some individuals appear to be natural-born networkers. However, according to Dr. Ivan Misner (founder of BNI - Business Network International), "Good networking is an acquired skill and one that not all people have acquired." While we are inherently social beings, networking prowess does not come automatically.

Through training and practice, you can develop and hone your networking abilities. It is essential to evaluate your motivations for connecting with new individuals at events. If you solely aim to secure new clients, you may be setting yourself up for disappointment. Instead, if your goal is to cultivate a network of Advocates – people who will actively recommend and support you – you are on the path to networking success.

A network comprises a series of interconnected nodes, each extending its reach through branching connections. In a business network, these nodes represent people – including you. As a contributing member of the network, you both receive and provide benefits by connecting one individual to another, facilitating the flow of information.

For example, a business owner with exceptional products that solve customers' problems may decide to expand their business through networking. Joining a local chamber of commerce, which hosts regular networking events, may seem like an ideal starting point. However, if the business owner treats these events as an advertising platform and fails to contribute to the network, their efforts to broaden their reach will be fruitless. A more effective approach is to understand others' offerings, and then act as a connector, linking those with needs to businesses that can resolve their issues.

The business owner's poor results at these events stem from their singular focus on finding an audience of prospects. Instead, the attendees could have become advocates; but each contact made at the event ended up as a dead-end, leaving the company's network stagnant. The business's network could flourish if the owner attended events with the intent of forging connections with individuals who could become advocates – those willing to recommend the company and its products or services. Investing time and resources in building advocates is a prudent move, as it is an investment in the company's future.

I commend you for choosing to develop your skills and build a network of advocates. By setting aside time to learn the art of Motivational Listening and effectively using this skill to establish rapport with others, you are on your way to becoming a successful networker.

Confronting Our Greatest Fear: Irrelevance

In 1964, the movie "The 7 Faces of Dr. Lao" was released, featuring a traveling circus arriving at an old west town. The film consists of several vignettes in which the townspeople interact with the circus members, each addressing a different issue. Although campy and formulaic, one particular vignette stands out for its poignancy.

A woman in the town, full of self-importance, with dreams of wealth, status, and power. Even though she possesses none of these, she treats others poorly and decides to have her fortune read by "Apollonius of Tyana". Expecting a reflection of her own aspirations, she is met with harsh truths instead. Apollonius reveals that her life will be full of "useless vanities," and that her existence will ultimately have no impact on the world.

He goes on to say, "Tomorrow will be like today, and the day after tomorrow will be like the day before yesterday. Your remaining days will be a tedious collection hours full of useless vanities. You will think no new thoughts, and you will forget what little you have known. Older you will become, but not wiser. Stiffer but not more dignified. When you die, you will be buried and forgotten. And for all the good or evil, creation or destruction your living might have accomplished, you might just as well have never lived at all."

This story highlights our greatest fear: irrelevance. The prospect of living an empty life, alone and insignificant, is deeply unsettling. We all know people like the woman in this vignette, whose lives seem devoid of purpose or meaning.

Merely existing is not enough.

In the previous chapter, we discussed the "hit & run" individual at a networking event, who haphazardly distributes business cards without establishing any real connections. To this person, others are mere targets, and their feelings of irrelevance are palpable.

It is not the responsibility of the recipient to decipher how the "hit & run" individual can help them. If the person took the time to genuinely connect, opportunities for collaboration or referral might arise. Instead, their approach leaves them effectively invisible, rendering their attendance at the event irrelevant.

Our inclination to choose the path of least resistance can lead to missed opportunities and feelings of dissatisfaction. Studies have shown that, when presented with two options, individuals often opt for the easier choice but later express regret for not having taken on a more challenging task. This inherent tendency can manifest in networking situations when people either avoid engaging in conversations or only interact with those they already know. Choosing the easy route may lead to regret over missed opportunities.

In this book, I focus on networking and the importance of connecting with others in a meaningful way. Overcoming the fear of irrelevance involves actively engaging with people, validating their worth, and genuinely investing in the relationships we build. By doing so, we can create a network of individuals who not only enrich our lives but also contribute to our professional and personal growth.

"If it was easy...."

Mastering the Art of Networking: Embracing Challenges and Overcoming Intimidation

Networking is far from easy. Even with a solid process for getting to know people and numerous events under your belt, walking into a room full of strangers can still be intimidating.

Consider this statement: "If it was easy..."

We often hear people claim that if something were easy, everyone would do it. But is that really true? Let's test this hypothesis with a simple game.

In my career as an entrepreneur, I have had the opportunity to explore various ventures, which not only allowed me to hone my networking skills but also fueled my creative spirit. One such endeavor was co-founding a game company with a team of imaginative and driven individuals. Our shared vision was to develop a physical board game that would bring people together, spark their creativity, and foster a sense of camaraderie.

As a co-founder, one of my primary responsibilities was to design different ways to play the game, essentially allowing me to tap into my creative side and develop innovative game concepts. This experience of creating games from scratch allowed me to understand the importance of engagement, interaction, and connection – all crucial elements in the world of networking.

Business Networking

Drawing from my background as an entrepreneur and game creator, I can illustrate the significance of making networking events more engaging and memorable, much like a well-designed board game. By tapping into our creativity, we can transform networking experiences into opportunities for authentic connection and collaboration.

Imagine a game in which you have a number of ping-pong balls and a large metal can. The objective is to toss the balls one at a time into the can as quickly as possible, and you will be timed. If the can is placed right next to you, the game becomes incredibly easy—simply dropping the balls into the can in a matter of seconds. This version of the game would likely bore you, as there is no challenge involved.

Now, if the can is placed on the other side of the room and you must bounce the balls off the floor and into the can, the game becomes more difficult. As you throw the balls, you learn their flight path, bounce, and the best technique for success. Once you've mastered the skill, you may want to play again to improve your score or even invite others to compete with you. In this case, the challenge makes the game more engaging and enjoyable.

Consider the parallels between a successful networking event and an immersive board game. Both require strategic thinking, effective communication, and the ability to adapt to different scenarios. Moreover, each demands a level of creativity and imagination that can only be achieved by stepping out of our comfort zones and embracing the challenges that come our way.

So, let's rephrase our initial statement: "If it was easy, nobody would do it."

Humans are wired to seek challenges. From the moment we're born, we need obstacles to overcome in order to grow and develop. For instance, when a baby is delivered via cesarean section, doctors make a small incision and ensure the baby experiences similar pressure as if passing through the birth canal. This pressure clears the lungs of fluid, allowing the child to breathe air for the first time and preventing a condition called "wet lung."

Challenges are essential for our survival and well-being, but they must have meaning. In one prison, an inmate was forced to move a pile of gravel from one end of the yard to the other each day. His punishment wasn't the physical labor, but rather the realization that his efforts were ultimately meaningless – his existence was irrelevant.

The fear of irrelevance is greater than the fear of pain, loss, or hard work. Many people attend networking events without reaping any benefits, feeling like the prisoner moving gravel from one event to the next. They may question their value or feel insignificant.

We have delved into the notion that facing challenges is crucial for our personal growth, survival, and overall well-being. By analyzing the brain activity of a volunteer engaged in a challenging game, we would likely uncover some fascinating discoveries.

First, engaging in challenging activities stimulates various areas of the brain, promoting the formation of new neural connections and strengthening existing ones. This process is crucial for cognitive development, problem-solving abilities, and adaptability. The more we expose our brains to challenges, the more adept we become at handling complex situations and learning new skills.

Second, during challenging activities, the brain releases chemicals such as dopamine and serotonin, which are associated with feelings of pleasure, motivation, and reward. These chemicals reinforce our desire to overcome obstacles and achieve goals, thus making us more resilient in the face of adversity.

Third, participating in challenging activities can also lead to a state of "flow" – a mental state where one becomes completely absorbed in the task at hand, experiencing optimal focus and enjoyment. Flow is associated with increased creativity, productivity, and overall well-being.

In summary, analyzing the brain activity of a volunteer playing a challenging game would reveal that such experiences are not only vital for cognitive development but also contribute to our overall mental health and happiness. By embracing challenges, we not only become more resilient but also unlock our full potential, ultimately leading more fulfilling lives.

If you have had similar experiences, it is time to rethink your approach to networking. By embracing the challenge and seeking meaningful connections, you can overcome the intimidation and make the most of networking opportunities.

You Are Remarkable!

Unconscious Competence

Let me begin this section by emphasizing that you, my dear reader, are truly remarkable.

Frequently, when we develop a skill or expertise that may have taken years of dedication and hard work to acquire, we tend to internalize it as an inherent part of our identity. The science behind this phenomenon, known as "unconscious competence," explains that as we progress through various stages of learning, our abilities become ingrained to the point where we can execute them effortlessly, without conscious thought (we'll explore this concept more in-depth later).

As we reach this level of mastery, our extraordinary skills may no longer feel remarkable or special to us. Instead, we might fall into the trap of assuming that our expertise is common knowledge, undervaluing our own unique capabilities. This mindset can lead to a lack of appreciation for our talents and can prevent us from recognizing our own accomplishments.

However, for an observer, your capabilities are anything but common – they are, in fact, remarkable. It's essential to remember that our skills and expertise are the result of a long and arduous journey that involved learning, practice, and growth. What might seem like second nature to us now was once a mountain we had to climb, and it's crucial to acknowledge the progress we've made.

By recognizing our own remarkable abilities, we can begin to appreciate our own worth and the unique value we bring to the table. This self-awareness can foster a sense of confidence and pride in our achievements, allowing us to present ourselves more effectively in personal and professional situations. So, never underestimate your own capabilities – they are a testament to your dedication, perseverance, and growth, making you truly remarkable.

Take my friend, for example, who has owned his plumbing business for over three decades. When he completes a flawless installation, he doesn't step back, brush off his hands, and declare, "Well, that's quite remarkable!" But the truth is, it is remarkable. He wasn't born with the ability to order the right supplies or install them perfectly. He acquired these skills through attending classes, workshops, and seminars, observing and learning from others, and experiencing trial and error. This talent has become such an integral part of who he is that it feels as natural as taking a breath.

What he accomplishes is far from ordinary. He is remarkable!

Just like my plumber friend, you too are remarkable and have a wealth of valuable knowledge and experience to offer. By mastering the art of Motivational Listening, you can not only rediscover your own unique qualities but also employ these techniques at networking events to help others recognize their potential.

Using a series of simple and targeted questions, you'll guide the speaker to divulge details about their life, background, and journey. In return, you'll be called upon to share aspects of your own experiences to establish common ground and foster connections. Remember, time is often limited at networking events, making it crucial to learn about others and create lasting impressions quickly.

To be perceived as an interesting person, it's essential to shift your focus towards being genuinely interested in others. By showing curiosity and appreciation for their individuality, you not only make them feel valued, but also reveal your own remarkable nature. This approach can lead to deeper connections, more fulfilling interactions, and a better understanding of the people around you.

Active Listening

I mentioned that Motivational Listening goes beyond active listening. Motivational Listening utilizes the tools and skills of active listening, so in this chapter we review active listening skills.

Active listening is a process of hearing and responding to improve understanding of the message being delivered. In a networking event it can be easy to be distracted; people are moving around, you might be offered food or drinks. You might notice someone you know or want to talk with, which might pull your thoughts away from the conversation at hand.

Be polite, if you have entered one conversation, follow through until there is a natural break. When I attend networking events, I arrive with 5 business cards or fewer. It is not my goal to try to connect with every person in the room. If I am a speaker, then I will have a stack of cards available because I know I will not be able to talk with everyone, and the cards offer, as a placeholder, a source for connection after the event.

There are defined active listening techniques. They help ensure you receive the message transmitted by the other person, and they know you understand what they have said.

1 – Be present, stay focused, and pay attention to what they say and how they say it:

Give the speaker your undivided attention and avoid distractions. Observe their tone, expressions, and body language to fully understand their message. Concentrate on the content and emotions behind their words.

Name tags and business cards are wonderful – your first goal is to remember the person's name (it is such a wonderful sound to that person to hear their name). Provide your undivided attention. Pronounce their name correctly.

Do not think ahead in the conversation. If you are thinking about what you are going to say next, you cannot be listening. You are just waiting for your opportunity to speak without responding to the direction the conversation is moving. Put aside distracting thoughts. Do not be distracted by what's going on around you; you should not be listening to the other conversations.

2 – Use body language to show you are listening:

Maintain eye contact, nod in agreement or understanding, and lean slightly forward to show engagement. Keep your arms uncrossed, maintain an open posture, and use facial expressions that convey interest and empathy. Body language, including your gestures will have a huge effect on the speaker.

***A quick aside**: An intriguing experiment was carried out to study the impact of body language on the speaker. College students were instructed to maintain eye contact with their professor only when he moved to the left. As soon as the professor began moving back to the right, they were to break eye contact. Ultimately, the students managed to steer the professor towards the far left wall using just the power of body language.*

Use appropriate eye contact; looking someone in the face conveys a sincere demeanor. It is a little uncomfortable and not right to "lock eyes" with the speaker. There is a preferred spot to focus when looking at another person's face. Research indicates it is best to look just below their eye level, right between their eyes. This is the preferred spot for business occasions.

Use facial expressions appropriate to the content of what they are saying. If the conversation is happy, then smile; if what they say is funny, then go ahead and laugh a natural laugh.

Conversations about loss are difficult. I learned that when someone talks about the loss of a loved one, it is good to acknowledge the loss. I do not recommend saying you are sorry for the loss, rather, I have found it helpful to note that you feel for them, or that your heart is with them.

Your voice tone will also be important in the conversation – using your voice to show surprise, awe, or joy will let them know you are paying attention.

Be aware of your posture and what you are doing with your hands; I like to keep their business card or a program in my hands – this keeps me from crossing my arms or wanting to put my hands in my pockets.

There are many good courses to study body language – these are just a few of the fundamentals.

3 - Be part of the conversation:

Active listening involves engaging in the conversation by asking relevant questions, paraphrasing what the speaker has said to demonstrate understanding, and offering appropriate feedback. This encourages the speaker to share more and helps build rapport.

This is not an opportunity for the speaker to monologue. There are very appropriate times for you to speak while being a Motivational Listener. If you do not say anything, the speaker will never know if you are really paying attention or perhaps you are just thinking about hitting the hors d'oeuvres. More importantly, it is a critical part of the process that you share (a little) about yourself. Research shows people are more comfortable when others share when engaging in conversation.

When the speaker is talking, simple sounds may be enough to acknowledge them and let them know you are tracking with what they are saying (e.g. “uh hmm”, “ahh”, “oh my!”, “go on....”) Just keep it within your personality style and be authentic.

Offering a short rephrase of a point for clarity; putting it as a question allows them to validate your understanding. (e.g. “So, there were 6 people on the project, but just you and one engineer showed up to the presentation?”) Providing a summary of the key points will help you to remember the conversation after the networking event is over as well as letting the speaker know you have been paying attention.

Keep the conversation moving forward by using questions. There are two types of questions you want to use: Closed and Open. Closed questions result in a simple yes or no answer. They are perfect when you need specific information. “Would you like another cup of coffee?” Open questions lead to longer, detailed answers. “Tell about...” “How were you able to accomplish...” are good examples of open questions.

4 - It is not a debate:

When practicing active listening, refrain from interrupting the speaker or trying to prove your point. The goal is to understand their perspective, not to win an argument. Keep an open mind and avoid being defensive or judgmental.

You are not at this networking event to share your point of view and win an argument. When the speaker brings up a topic or opinion that is counter to yours – you are simply learning about them, it does not necessarily prevent them from being an advocate. If it appears the person is looking for debate then find a point to disengage and move on.

Allow the speaker to finish each point before asking questions. Don't interrupt with counter arguments.

5 - Respond do not React:

We all react. Reaction is a quick visceral comment or facial expression which is driven by emotion. We are emotional beings. We are also rational. Reaction is emotional; Responding is rational. At an event, when your goal is to get to know people and build a network, you want to take a measured approach.

When responding to the speaker, take a moment to think before you speak. This helps to avoid reacting impulsively or emotionally. Provide thoughtful feedback and ask clarifying questions to ensure that you have fully understood their message.

People will always have opinions to express. I'm reminded of a friend of mine who is professor at a university. He would start his classes at the beginning of the term by introducing himself and telling his students, "I have a lot of opinions, and they're all correct." Of course, his students would think the same thing you might be thinking right now as well. "That guy has some ego!" He would continue after a moment of pause, and he would ask his students, "Do any of you have opinions?" Of course they would indicate that yes, they do have opinions. He would then ask, "Well, how many of your opinions are wrong?" He paused to look at his students and say, "OK then, we have an understanding."

Your opinions are yours. It may be that, as you pursue Motivational Listening with the speaker, you note your opinion is different. In all of your conversations, be respectful. Respect will get you a long way toward your goal of building relationships and developing a network of advocates.

6 - Encourage the speaker:

Using verbal encouragements, like "I see," "Go on," or "Tell me more," is an effective way to signal your interest in a conversation and encourage the speaker to continue sharing their thoughts. These simple yet powerful expressions demonstrate that you are actively listening and genuinely engaged in what they have to say. By incorporating these phrases into your conversations, you can create a more open and comfortable atmosphere, fostering deeper connections and more meaningful exchanges with others.

7 - Practice empathy:

Making an effort to understand the emotions and feelings behind a speaker's words can be a powerful way to connect with them on a deeper level and validate their experiences. By empathizing with their perspective and tuning in to the emotions they express, you demonstrate that you truly care about their thoughts and feelings. This level of understanding can create a sense of trust and rapport, strengthening the bond between you and the speaker, and ultimately enriching the conversation as a whole.

8 - Summarize and reflect:

During a conversation, it's important to occasionally summarize the key points discussed and reflect back the speaker's feelings and emotions, especially at the end or when appropriate. This shows that you have been actively listening and engaged in the conversation. Moreover, by restating the main points and acknowledging their emotions, you confirm that you have correctly understood their message. This practice fosters clarity and prevents misunderstandings, while also validating the speaker's thoughts and feelings, further strengthening the connection between both parties.

9 - Be patient:

Giving the speaker enough time to gather their thoughts and express themselves is essential in a conversation. It's important to resist the urge to finish their sentences or interrupt with your own thoughts. By doing so, you demonstrate respect for their perspective and allow them the space they need to communicate effectively. This practice not only helps in building rapport but also ensures that the speaker feels heard and understood, contributing to a more meaningful and productive dialogue.

10 - Seek clarification:

When engaging in a conversation, it's crucial to seek clarification or further explanation if you are uncertain about something the speaker mentioned. By doing so, you demonstrate that you are actively trying to comprehend their message and taking their perspective seriously. This approach helps to prevent miscommunication and shows the speaker that you are genuinely interested in understanding their point of view, fostering a more open and effective dialogue.

Active Listening Summarized:

1 - Be present and pay attention

2 - Use body language to show you are listening

3 - Be part of the conversation

4 - It is not a debate

5 - Respond, don't react

6 - Encourage the speaker

7 - Practice empathy

8 - Summarize and reflect

9 - Be patient

10 - Seek clarification

By honing these active listening skills, you'll be better equipped to engage in meaningful conversations, foster deeper connections, and create an environment where everyone feels heard and understood.

Science of Relationships

In the "If it was easy..." section, we explored the idea that challenges are essential for our growth, survival, and overall well-being. If we were to examine the brain activity of a volunteer playing a challenging game, we would likely discover some intriguing insights.

Scientific research has made significant strides in recent years, giving us empirical evidence to better comprehend various phenomena. Among these advancements, tools like electroencephalograms (EEG) and functional magnetic resonance imaging (fMRI) have revolutionized the way we study the human brain.

EEGs measure electrical activity in the brain through small electrodes placed on the scalp, providing real-time data on brainwave patterns. This allows researchers to observe brain activity during different tasks, emotional states, and cognitive processes. EEGs are particularly useful for studying sleep, attention, and various neurological disorders.

fMRI, on the other hand, measures brain activity by detecting changes in blood flow associated with neuronal activity. When a brain region is more active, it consumes more oxygen, causing an increase in blood flow to that area. fMRI can create detailed maps of the brain and show which areas are engaged during specific tasks or when processing certain emotions. This technique has been pivotal in understanding the functional organization of the brain and how different regions interact with one another.

By employing these advanced tools, researchers can investigate the physiological responses of the brain under a wide range of conditions. This has led to groundbreaking discoveries in neuroscience, psychology, and cognitive science, helping us gain a deeper understanding of human behavior, emotions, and thought processes. These insights have practical applications in areas such as mental health, education, and even the development of new technologies like brain-computer interfaces.

If we were to place our game-playing volunteer inside an fMRI machine while they attempt to toss the ball into the can, we would be able to observe specific brain areas being activated when they succeed. When the volunteer achieves their goal, there would be a release of neurotransmitters and hormones, such as dopamine, which triggers a surge of pleasure as a reward for accomplishing a task.

Interestingly, the brain's reward system doesn't solely activate when we achieve success; it also responds when we come close to it. For example, if the ball nearly made it into the can and bounced off the edge, the same brain areas would be activated, albeit to a lesser extent, as if the throw had been successful. This near-miss effect can motivate us to continue trying, as our brains anticipate the rewarding feeling that comes with eventual success.

This phenomenon highlights the intricate workings of the human brain and how it responds to challenges and achievements. By understanding these processes, we can better comprehend our motivations and the role our brain plays in reinforcing behaviors that lead to goal attainment. Moreover, it emphasizes the importance of perseverance and determination, as even near misses can stimulate our brain's reward system and drive us to keep trying.

The feeling of success is indeed invigorating, providing us with a sense of accomplishment and fulfillment. Intriguingly, near success can be just as stimulating. When we come close to achieving our goals, our brain's reward system is activated, creating a desire to keep going and experience that pleasurable sensation once more.

This near success effect is a powerful motivational force, as it compels us to persist in our efforts despite not yet reaching our intended objectives. The anticipation of the eventual reward, along with the excitement of nearly achieving it, spurs us to continue striving for success.

In essence, both success and near success contribute to our drive for achievement, reinforcing our determination and tenacity. By recognizing and embracing these feelings, we can harness their motivational power to overcome obstacles and maintain our pursuit of personal and professional goals. This understanding of the impact of near success on our motivation highlights the importance of perseverance, resilience, and a growth mindset, which are essential qualities for overcoming challenges and achieving success in the long run.

So these scientific tools (EEG, fMRI, etc.) add to our understanding of human behavior. The brain can be understood (to a limited extent, we have much to learn about the operations of the human brain).

This is a tremendous advancement.

You see, in the first half of the last century the emphasis was on Behaviorism, that is, Behavior is a simple series of Inputs & Outputs, of Stimuli & Response resulting in "conditioning". You might remember Pavlov and his drooling dogs. The dominant thought was that external forces controlled behavior and free will did not exist. You brain was simply a "Black Box".

In college I took a class called, "Experimental Psychology", affectionately known as "Rat Lab". We had our test subject – a cute little white rat named Sylvester. We attempted to manage his behavior through conditioning. We would change the inputs (stimuli) and document his response (output). We were moderately successful in changing his behavior by associating an outcome with a stimulus.

Behaviorism was developed by scientist John Watson in 1913 (expanding on Pavlov's conditioning). He conducted a famous experiment where he had a baby touch a rat; and all was fine, the child was not afraid. Then each time the child touched the rat, Watson banged a hammer on the table. The baby became terrified and connected the experience of being startled (frightened by the loud sound) with touching the rat. The child connected fear to the rat and, indeed, all furry creatures. This was accomplished by associating an outcome with a stimulus.

The work on Behaviorism was continued by B.F. Skinner who denied that the mind (or that feelings) have any impact; you see, Behaviorism wanted to not only understand human behavior, but to *predict and control* it, even without understanding the processes within the brain. These scientists did not have the tools to understand the physical workings of the brain to the extent we have today.

We might like to have a simple equation for dealing with other people. However, none of us can be reduced to a series of stimuli and responses.

We are complex creatures. Our brain behaves like no other. What other beast would look for a challenge? We demonstrated the need for challenge in our game-experiment with the balls and metal can. What else can we know by looking at the brain?

You were not designed to be alone; we are social creatures. This is beneficial, because the goal of this book is to equip you to venture into a social situation where you might not know even ONE person. There is good news: Studies confirm that our brains are wired for connection and social interaction. Much of the early research focused on romantic relationships. More recently, we have examined friendship.

Robert Louis Stevenson said, "*A friend is a gift you give yourself.*" A more intimate perspective is Aristotle when asked to define friendship – he said, "*A single soul dwelling in two bodies.*"

Here is what we know about relationships: If you have good social connections, you have better health and live longer.

You might think the obvious answer is practical support - such as sharing food or work. We call this "Enacted Support". But it turns out "Perceived Support" is more important. Perceived Support is the knowledge that your friends and family will "be there for you".

Clinical psychologist Jim Coan conducted a study where he placed an individual in a scanner so he could see what was happening inside their brain when the person was shown images. Nothing would happen when the subject saw a Blue "O"; however, when a Red "X" appeared there was a 20% chance of receiving a mild electric shock on the ankle.

His study was focused on hand-holding, and we know that physical touch can release Oxytocin (another chemical produced in our bodies – Oxytocin is linked to feelings of contentment, reduced anxiety, calmness, and security. Some call Oxytocin the "trust molecule"). So part of the test had the subject holding the hand of a loved-one, a stranger, or to be by themselves with no one holding their hand.

When the Red "X" appeared, the brain went wild in anticipation of the potential shock, the "fight-or-flight" response would activate. The Hypothalamus portion of the subject's brain began releasing stress hormones. When the subject had someone with them their brain was calmer, even without the holding of hands. Closer relationships were more calming, but even being with a stranger made the situation more manageable. We can conclude that alone the world is more daunting.

Another study on friendship involved placing the person at the base of a hill and asking them to estimate how steep the climb would be to reach the top. Invariably the hill was not perceived to be as steep when they had a friend next to them. The friend did not even need to be physically present. The subject was asked to just think of a good friend and the steepness of the hill was considered to be less than when the subject was alone.

You are going into a social situation to meet new people and build your network of advocates. The good news: Those people at the event want to connect with you.

In the next chapter we will look at what happens in the brain when we are learning and practical tools to use when connecting at networking events.

Your Brain: Neuroplasticity (Lifelong Learning)

Neuroplasticity mean that your brain continues to develop. When you do something new or are learning, this occurs in your Prefontal Cortex. This is a where we house short-term memory, and it takes a lot of energy. You burn off glucose (the sugar in your blood) feeding your brain. Recall that your brain will use 20% of the energy you produce. While reading this book you are learning how to optimize your networking skills and using your prefrontal cortex. This use of energy is one reason when you go to an all-day seminar and then get into bed that night that you are physically tired. It is because you have been using the high-energy portion of your brain and used much of the energy you produced that day.

As tasks are repeated they become routine and new neural pathways are formed in your brain. The information moves from your Prefontal Cortex to the Basal Ganglia. Tasks which once required a lot of attention seem automatic.

Take the example of learning how to drive. When you first started to drive, there was so much to think about. You had to remember to keep your hands on the wheel, check the mirrors, watch your speed, and much more. You did not want to turn on the radio or talk. You needed to concentrate.

Now you walk out to your car sit down, you do not have to look where the key goes or think, "Do I turn it to the left or right to start the car?" When you drive home at the end of the day, there may be a four-way stop between your office and home. Did you stop? You may be pretty certain you stopped, but you do not quite remember. This is because you are working out of your long-term, hard-wired memory.

We have discussed two sections of the brain: Prefrontal Cortex (learning and short-term memory) and the Basal Ganglia (long-term memory). There is one more portion that is very important to understand relative to Motivational Listening, that is the Orbito-frontal Cortex, a little understood portion of the brain. Fortunately for us, the amount of research in the past few years has been increasing and tools like the EEG and fMRI are giving us a better view of this area located just above your eye sockets, which is activated by such diverse stimulants as touch, taste, smell, and even winning and losing money. We will learn more in the next chapter.

Daydreaming, Theory of Mind, and Emotional Intelligence

Daydreaming:

We spend one third to one half of our waking hours daydreaming. Daydreaming! Seems unreal, yet there is solid research around the topic; however, daydreaming is not the subject of this course, just that we want to be aware that when you are at a networking event, it is a natural occurrence for people to lose focus on the situation; daydreaming is an altered state of consciousness and pulls attention away from our cognitive functions.

A quick aside: There is benefit in studying and learning to direct your daydreams; research indicates you can be happier and even improve your memory when your daydreams are on familiar, local, and attainable topics.

Back to networking. At an event, we want to ensure we are pulling the speaker into the conversation and away from daydreaming. As we approach and engage an individual, we what to activate their cognitive functions.

A part of your frontal lobes and located right above your eye sockets is the Orbito-frontal Cortex (OFC). When you are optimizing your effectiveness at networking events, it is helpful to understand some of how the OFC plays an active role in both you and the speaker. In the last chapter, I mentioned this area of the brain was activated by touch, taste, smell, and even when something deviates from the expected (which is quite important in Motivational Listening as we connect at networking events, more about that later). We know what activates the OFC; what it is responsible for is quite amazing.

The OFC is responsible for face and voice recognition, and for comparative prediction which allows us to adapt behavior in response to unexpected rewards or adversity – and in turn, follow the course leading to reward (instead of punishment). This little part of our incredible brain also facilitates empathy.

We are now really getting down to why Motivational Listening is so effective for networking.

Theory of Mind:

Dr. Simon Moss notes, "To socialize effectively, individuals need to understand the perspectives and preferences of other people. They need to appreciate the feelings and accommodate the desires of another person." This capacity is called "Theory of Mind". The orbito-frontal cortex facilitates this capacity.

We have two distinct aspects of the Theory of Mind which have been classified and studied:

Cognitive theory of mind: which allows us to appreciate another's beliefs, assumptions, and motivations (we will talk more about motivation later because it is a critical goal of Motivational Listening).

Affective theory of mind: giving us the ability to appreciate the emotions and feelings of others (this is that aspect of empathy, which is also facilitated by the OFC).

The cognitive and affective aspects of the Theory of Mind often work in conjunction but serve different purposes.

The cognitive theory of mind is fundamentally concerned with one's ability to understand the mental states of others, such as thoughts, beliefs, desires, and intentions, and to predict or explain others' actions based on these mental states.

This capacity, which usually develops around age 4 or 5 in typical development, is critical for successful social interactions and communication. It's the cognitive aspect of Theory of Mind that lets us understand that people have perspectives and knowledge that might differ from our own and that these differences can influence their actions.

The affective theory of mind, on the other hand, is related to our capacity to understand and respond to others' emotional states. It's about recognizing and empathizing with the emotions that others are experiencing. Affective theory of mind is closely linked to empathy and involves not just understanding others' emotional states but also responding to them in a socially appropriate way. For example, if a friend is sad, the affective theory of mind enables us to recognize their sadness, understand its cause, and provide comfort.

While both cognitive and affective aspects of the Theory of Mind are essential for social interactions, they focus on different aspects of our understanding of others. Cognitive theory of mind helps us understand what others might think or believe, while the affective theory of mind helps us understand how others might feel. Together, these two aspects of Theory of Mind enable us to navigate complex social environments and interactions, from maintaining friendships to collaborating with colleagues or resolving conflicts. Both require the ability to step out of one's own perspective and into someone else's, and both are facilitated by the orbito-frontal cortex, although they also rely on other brain regions such as the temporo-parietal junction and the amygdala.

When we talked about Behaviorism, we noted an outcome was associated with a stimulus. Such tools as the fMRI and EEG allow us to see it is a *physiological* process, at least partially rooted in the functioning of the OFC. During networking events, we want to activate the OFC through a series of intentional steps to engage the speaker's cognitive functions. We want to build a favorable connection and associate with you. It is a positive use of stimulus and outcome.

Emotional Intelligence:

Emotional Intelligence is the ability to recognize and differentiate emotions and to keep feelings from ruling you. The concept of emotional intelligence was introduced in 1990 by Peter Salovey (Yale) and John Mayer (University of New Hampshire).

There has been a fair amount of research and popular writings on the topic; and, you may have heard of the term EQ or Emotional Quotient. This is derived from standardized testing that has been developed to attempt to measure an individual's ability to read emotions. Some of the research indicates that EQ is a better predictor of long-term life success than IQ (intelligence quotient). I will leave that to the academic world for now.

There are three skills the emotionally intelligent utilize:

1 - They have emotional awareness of themselves and others;

2 - They are able to discern how they are feeling;

3 - They are able to regulate their own emotions and can influence others (e.g. cheer those who are feeling down, or calm down someone who is over-excited).

Those with good emotional intelligence are able to utilize their emotions and apply them to tasks such as problem solving. Research by William Killgore in 2017 (University of Arizona) describes two distinct definitions and measurement of Emotional Intelligence called Ability and Trait.

Ability Emotional Intelligence can be likened to an Intelligence Quotient. The measurement test for this was developed by the scientists who first described the subject (Salovey, Mayer, and Caruso). The emphasis is on demonstrated knowledge and performance to measure emotional reasoning and problem solving. Four areas of observation are: 1. Perceiving emotions; 2. Facilitating emotions; 3. Understanding emotions; and, 4. Managing emotions.

Trait Emotional Intelligence is defined as a set of self-perceptions and dispositions. The best measure is through introspection and self-assessment. The common test for this is the Bar-On test (1997) and is referred to as EQi. The five traits examined are: 1. Intrapersonal (self); 2. Interpersonal (between others); 3. Stress management; 4. Adaptability; and, 5. General mood.

It is helpful to note there are assessments available. I do not necessarily recommend seeking a testing facility to measure your personal emotional intelligence unless you intend to follow with a program to improve upon any score received. I have a strong bias toward only measuring that which you are able and willing to change.

That being said, there is information available to improve or strengthen your emotional intelligence. Generally speaking, the best way to become better at something is to "just do it". Here are eight steps you can take to be better with emotional intelligence:

1 - Daily: be aware of your emotional changes

2 - Take time to write down emotional changes

3 - Note if/how you were able to manage or change your emotions

4 - State your emotions in third person (e.g. one of my emotions is frustration)

5 - Note if there was a positive or negative impact relative to the emotion changing or remaining the same

6 - Note if you can accurately "read" the emotions of another person

7 - If necessary, were you able to influence the emotions of another person

8 - Remember, we are both emotional and rational creatures. Utilize the rational side to accept emotions as data which can be analyzed and utilized

When at networking events, there is a ton going on...plenty of noise, other conversations, people moving around, perhaps bumping into you. It is incumbent on you to focus on the speaker, paying close attention to what is being communicated. You must listen to the words and tone, as well the non-audio portion of the message including gestures and micro-expressions.

Gestures are important in a cultural context, that is, the way we talk with our hands is a learned behavior. In a social environment you gain a certain amount of information from these gestures, however, it is not as conclusive as micro-expressions.

Micro-expressions are momentary changes to the face based on a specific emotion. Paul Ekman (UC San Francisco) and Dacher Keltner (UC Berkeley) have researched the subject. There are seven emotions which are a universally demonstrated by these micro-expressions. I say "universally" because they cross cultures and experience. It is, apparently, hard-wired into our bodies.

The seven micro-expressions exhibiting emotions are:

1 - Fear

2 - Sadness

3 - Anger

4 - Disgust

5 - Happiness

6 - Surprise

7 - Contempt

The body reacts to emotions – changes in heart rate, blood flow to the muscles, finger temperature, and more. Each of these emotions has a set of facial configurations which communicate the emotional state. In the case of our networking event, it is our speaker. When you are engaged with the speaker and building rapport, and paying attention to emotional micro-expressions, they have the ability to affect you as well. You can experience increased heart-rate and blood flow. Remember, the emotionally intelligent recognize, control, and utilize their emotions. Use these emotions to connect with the speaker.

Here is a description of the facial changes we see for each of the emotions:

Fear: Eyes getting big with the upper white showing; the eyebrows will go up then down; the lower lip is pulled down and the mouth opens; the face skin may grow paler as blood is withdrawn; and, sweat can form on the forehead.

Sadness: The corners of the mouth become depressed, pulling down, and the lower lip may even quiver; the eyebrows are squished together; the skin around the eyes is pulled in, and tears may start to form.

Anger: Eyebrows are pushed down and together, two lines are formed between them; the corners of the mouth are turned down; Nostrils are standing out and the nose is wrinkled; eyes bulge and put tension on the eyelids; and, the lips are tightly pursed.

Disgust: The nose wrinkles, cheeks are raised, the lower lids are raised, and the upper lip is raised.

Happiness: The forehead is relaxed with slight wrinkles as the eyebrows are slightly raised; the corners of the mouth are curling up, and the cheeks are lifted; there are lines from the outer nose to the outer mouth; when the emotion is genuine, the outer corners of the eyes will slightly wrinkle in a way that is quite difficult to fake.

Surprise: Eyebrows are pulled up high, making the eyes open wide (showing the whites of the eyes); the eyebrows are curved in an arch; the forehead is wrinkled; and, the mouth is opens as the jaw relaxes.

Contempt: The lop-sided smile; it is that smirk when one corner of the mouth is raised, and they eyes squint a little.

I put Surprise and Contempt at the end of the list because there is some academic debate as to whether these are a part of the universal micro-expression. We do not have to be concerned about whether or not they ought to be included in the list of micro-expressions. Surprise and Contempt will be present at networking events.

Micro-expressions are not lightly named, they only last one-half of a second or less. In crowded and noisy rooms, you may not be able to hear every word or clearly hear the tone, but you can see these cues to emotion when you are paying attention to the speaker.

Now that we have all the pieces, we can look at how you pull them all together to be a Motivational Listener.

Networking: Brain Science Summary

We noted at the beginning of the book that the goal of being a Motivational Listener is for the speaker to exit the conversation feeling better about themselves than when they entered. We have looked at research in neuroscience to find details on the inner workings of our brains and how it facilitates human connection. We will apply these learning to intentionally build rapport with others in unfamiliar situations.

Networking is about building advocates; extending your network of people who are willing to support or endorse you publically.

Our greatest fear is Irrelevance; we need meaningful challenges. Existence is not enough.

Remember: You are Remarkable! You have worked hard to obtain knowledge, skill, and expertise. What you have to offer is valuable.

Active Listening skills are important when building rapport at networking events. These skills are:

1 - Be present and pay attention

2 - Use body language to show you are listening

3 - Be part of the conversation

4 - It is not a debate

5 - Respond, do not react

In the Science of Relationships we saw that we are happier and healthier when we have good relationships. That friendships do not require physical presence; and, that there is a blurring of lines between self and other. We will take actions to protect others as we would ourselves – a threat to a friend is a threat to us.

Neuroplasticity: new neuropathways form in our brain when we repeat tasks. What once took a lot of energy has now routine and takes very little brain work. This is good for efficiency, but causes us to forget the value we offer. We may feel like what we know is common knowledge. It is not.

Daydreaming: We spend between one third to one half of our waking hours in daydreaming. Just a fact.

Theory of Mind:

Cognitive Theory of Mind: which allows us to appreciate another's beliefs, assumptions, and motivations.

Affective Theory of Mind: giving us the ability to appreciate the emotions and feelings of others (this is that aspect of empathy, which is also facilitated by the OFC).

Emotional Intelligence: the ability to recognize and differentiate emotions and to keep feelings from ruling you.

1 - They have emotional awareness of themselves and others;

2 - They are able to discern how they are feeling;

3 - They are able to regulate their own emotions, and they can influence others (cheer those who are feeling down, or calm down someone who is over-excited).

There are seven micro-expressions, changes in the face which last for one-half second or less; they are: Fear, Sadness, Anger, Disgust, Happiness, Surprise, and Contempt.

Becoming a Motivational Listener

Business networking is about building advocates – those who are willing to refer and support you and your solutions in public. As a Motivational Listener, your goal is not to spend time talking about yourself. The goal is to help the speaker feel better about themselves following your conversation.

We have set a foundation, now we look at the practical steps of being a Motivational Listener:

1. Activate Cognitive Functions (Orbito-frontal Cortex)

2. Guide them on a conversational Journey

3. Utilize Emotional Intelligence to monitor the conversation

4. Differentiate Result and Motivation

5. Summarize and let them know they are Remarkable

6. Close by asking for contact information and permission to follow up

Business Networking

I have been to countless networking events. When I entered the event with a plan and purpose, I left feeling successful. Attending events without a plan is a waste of your most valuable resource – you will never recover the time spent. Walking into a room full of strangers with a plan and the skills of a Motivational Listener will add value to your business and career.

Prior to moving into the details on each step in the process of being a Motivational Listener I want to set the stage for your mindset and expectations. The development of a network of advocates takes time and the results will not be evident in the short term.

I will start with Goals then give you a framework of Motivation Theory.

Goal Setting

Gail Matthews (Dominican University) conducted testing around how to achieve goals. There are five levels, each resulting in a higher probability that you will successful.

1. **Have Goals:** It seems simplistic, and maybe you would not be surprised at how few people actually have goals. The first step in success at networking is to have goals;

2. **Put Your Goals in Writing:** This allows you to periodically review your goals and refresh you activities to meet them. Networking goals could include the number of events attended or relationships built;

3. **Develop a Plan to Meet Your Goals:** Having a plan will improve the probability of success. Your network goals could include having a specific number of industry and out of industry contacts by a certain time by attending named events, shows, or mixers;

4. **Share Your Goals with Another Person:** My wife will remind me, "What is clear to me is clear to me." When we explain our goals to someone, we have to be able to communicate to then what we intend to achieve. And, they must understand what we are attempting. This process clarifies what we intend when building our network;

5. **Seek Accountability:** This is the most invasive step in being successful in building your network. When you have someone who will keep you accountable to attend events and be a Motivational Listener to build your network, the pressure is on!

These practical goal-setting steps will support your efforts in building a network of advocates. It does take effort and you will need to maintain a level of motivation to be successful.

Motivation Theory

Motivation theory is an essential part of psychology that aims to understand what drives individuals to behave the way they do. In the context of skill acquisition, motivation plays a key role as it propels the individual to learn and master new skills, be it becoming a motivational listener or a skilled networker.

Ruth Kanfer, a prominent researcher in this field from the Georgia Institute of Technology, has contributed significantly to our understanding of motivation theory. Kanfer's work focuses on how individual differences, self-regulation, and motivation contribute to work performance. Her theories of motivation are centered around the concept of "goal-directed behavior." In essence, she suggests that people's actions are guided by their goals, and the individual's motivation influences the effort they put in to achieve these goals.

In the context of skill acquisition, this means that a person's motivation to learn a new skill, such as motivational listening or networking, will influence how much effort they put into learning and mastering that skill. If someone is highly motivated to become a good listener, for instance, they will likely spend more time practicing listening skills, seek out feedback, and make a concerted effort to improve.

Motivation theory also underscores the importance of intrinsic motivation - the inherent desire to engage in a behavior because it is enjoyable or satisfying in some way, rather than because of external rewards or outcomes.

Intrinsic motivation is often a stronger and more sustainable driving force than extrinsic motivation, which is driven by external rewards or outcomes. For example, someone who is intrinsically motivated to become a skilled networker may find the process of meeting new people and building relationships rewarding in itself, and thus may be more likely to persist in their efforts even in the absence of immediate external rewards.

Despite the limited recent research in motivation theory, it continues to be a crucial area of study. Understanding what motivates people can help in various fields, from education to organizational behavior, by informing strategies to enhance learning, performance, and overall productivity. It also has profound implications for personal development and self-improvement, as recognizing and harnessing our motivations can empower us to acquire new skills and achieve our goals.

Let me define these three motivation components to allow you to see how you can affect motivation to succeed at networking:

1 - **Direction:** Deciding what to do, when to do it, and when to quit

2 - **Intensity:** The level of effort exerted in any particular Direction

3 - **Persistence:** How long or often will you continue in a direction (indicative of patterns of behavior)

How intentional you go about building your network is your choice (Direction). You determine the level of effort (Intensity) and how many events you attend (Persistence). This is important because you will have events which "fail", that is, you do not make any meaningful contacts.

We have all wanted to motivate ourselves an others to take certain actions. Often rewards are Extrinsic – some external reward provided following a task. Examples are sales commissions or sports trophies. Research tells us such tangible rewards can be detrimental when the motivation is Intrinsic. Intrinsic motivation spurs us to engage in a task or behavior for its own sake. I mentioned the "payoff" for building each individual contact and your network of advocates will take time. If the reward is extrinsic, such as a new client or referral, the motivation to sustain the effort will not last.

You can set short-term goals with a long-term vision. Your vision is a robust network of those willing to promote you publically and send referrals to you as you send referrals to your advocates. The vision will be realized through a series of short-term goals and habits. The habits will develop as you repeat the six steps of being a Motivational Listener. Your initial goals will be to attend a networking event and implement the six steps once. After the event, review your experience (perhaps with an accountability partner).

Skill Acquisition

Intrinsic motivation is quite important when the realization of the vision will come in an undefined future or when the achievement of goals requires complex or new skills. The process of becoming an effective networker will require sustained effort.

Our intrinsic motivation is surrounded with several individual and interpersonal motivations. By naming and defining these aspects of motivation we are able to recognize the role they play in our networking effectiveness.

The four **Individual** Motivations are:

1 - **Challenge:** We are more likely to remain involved in tasks which present continuous and/or escalating intermediate levels of difficulty with personally meaningful goals. You can think back to the game of tossing balls into the can and our fear of irrelevance

2 - **Curiosity:** This is a force which grabs our attention for new knowledge and/or skills

3 - **Control:** We desire a measure of autonomy over our actions and choices

4 - **Fantasy:** Is the mental images that simulate a future state, perhaps a having a robust network of advocates

You can see how these reflect what was discussed earlier in the book. Individual motivations are present when we choose to attend networking events.

The three **Interpersonal** Motivations are:

1 - **Competition:** Comparing our performance with that of others

2 - **Cooperation:** Satisfaction helping others reach goals or achieving mutually desired results when combining complementary skills

3 - **Recognition:** This is a satisfaction we feel when others acknowledge and appreciate our efforts and achievements

The Individual and Interpersonal Motivations are all present at various times as you build a network.

Now we take this background information and apply it with the six steps of becoming a Motivational Listener. This process will instill you with confidence to take initiative in approaching new people. Your manner will be recognized as being a person with strong purpose and motivation. Your interactions with those you meet will cause them to be inspired.

In closing this chapter, we looked at the fundamental roles that individual and interpersonal motivations play in networking. By understanding these motivations, we become more effective in building and maintaining effective business relationships.

The four types of individual motivations identified - Challenge, Curiosity, Control, and Fantasy - help us to engage in tasks and strive for goals that are personally meaningful. Whether it's the challenge of a difficult task, seeking new knowledge, the desire for autonomy, or envisioning a future state, each of these motivations can be found in our decisions to attend networking events and engage with others.

Similarly, our interactions with others are also influenced by three interpersonal motivations: Competition, Cooperation, and Recognition. We find satisfaction in comparing our performance to others, assisting in the achievement of common goals, and receiving acknowledgment for our efforts. These forces are present as we navigate the social landscape of networking.

The concepts of individual and interpersonal motivations align with what has been discussed in this book. By understanding and harnessing these motivations, we are equipped to become 'Motivational Listeners' – individuals who not only listen but inspire others through our interactions.

The six steps of becoming a Motivational Listener, when combined with a clear understanding of our motivations, fill us with the confidence to approach new people, displaying a strong sense of purpose. Our manner, backed by this awareness and confidence, will inspire those we meet.

Motivational Listener Step 1 – Activate Cognitive Functions

The first thing we are going to do is to "Test the waters".

Not every person is going to be receptive to connecting. I know it seems odd. Here they are at a networking event, and they are not interested in talking? There could be many reasons for this: they are not feeling well, or they have some pressing issue rolling around their head, or they are just happy snacking at the buffet. No problem, there are plenty of people to meet.

I want to differentiate the process for approaching a person by themselves (that is, they are not engaged with another person) and groups (a group is any number greater than one, where some amount of conversation is taking place).

We start with the single individual not engaged in a conversation. This will give us the basic tool-set to build rapport and be interesting by being interested.

How to Approach the Lone Person:

The purpose of the event is to connect, yet it may feel strange to simply approach someone standing or sitting by themselves. It is certainly not something we do just out in public. Here it is safe to do so.

When you reach out to a lone person, you are not going to lead with your name and an outstretched hand itching for a handshake. Nor will the first thing you do is to ask for the person's name or present them with a cliché question such as, "How are you?"

We just want to gage if that person is open to talking. Remember, they are just like you. They may feel a bit awkward at initial contact with someone they do not know. Your approach will open the opportunity to make an introduction feel natural. We want to allow them to move comfortably into a conversation with us. It is best to open with a statement, broad and non-threatening.

Some simple statements can focus on the venue, food, number of people at the event, compare the weather outside to the comfort of being inside. If the event is outside, comment on the view, landscaping, or the beauty of the clouds. The important part is to have your statement open to a positive response. You never, NEVER want to go negative. You are making a first impression, make it a positive experience. What you are hoping, is that you get them to make a positive response back to your statement. Let me run some specific statements past you.

We start with the venue: "This room is really beautiful; the organizers certainly did an outstanding work on the decorations."

These types of statements allow the person to respond in agreement – or if they are not interested, you will be able to tell. You have not committed to a long discussion with them. If you start with your name, there is an expectation to share what you do for work, and the same for them. This will be awkward if the conversation should not be continued (not all conversations should be extended).

Talk about food: Keep it positive. If you have nothing good to say, find another opening statement. Good ways to start, "They are very generous with the food...I won't be needing breakfast after this!"; "Not only is the food great, the presentation is really nice." Even if you are not going to eat anything (perhaps there is only dessert). You can say, "Those desserts are so tempting, I may have to smuggle some home to the kids."

In each statement you make, you are presenting a non-personal, non-threatening opportunity for the person to agree with you. They may respond with a similar positive comment opening an opportunity for you to continue the process of Motivational Listening. If you get the right feeling (engaging your Emotional Intelligence), you can move to the next step. In this book, however, our next topic is approaching people in groups.

Connecting with a Person in a Group:

Connecting with an individual that is a part of an existing group conversation is more of a challenge than a lone individual and will require patience.

Often you may have a specific person you want to connect with; when you are going to a networking event that has a published guest list – perhaps a convention or trade show – you can do your homework ahead of time and identify the individuals you want to meet.

Learn what you can through the company website (or their personal site) using LinkedIn, Twitter or other social channels, which can give you an insight into that person. Learn what you can about their background, education, interests, and so forth.

If you want to connect with a famous person, it is important to do your homework. Did you read their book? Visit their website or read through their Blog? You want to be armed with something that is not already publically available, such as a question of clarification. It is embarrassing if it is obvious you are not prepared because of the questions you ask. Do your homework.

Back to the group.

Getting into a group is a challenge (but we live for challenge).

Look for a group that is not “overly intimate”. An intimate group is small consisting of 2-4 people that are in a tight circle, perhaps leaning-in to each other; they might reach out and touch another member’s arm or shoulder. It is likely you are not going to break into that group. Move on.

It is natural for a group of 3 or more to form a relatively close circle – they are not thinking about leaving an open spot for you to fill. You will have to be a bit bold. Remember, this is a networking event – everyone was a stranger at one point. They are not there to keep you out. Find a group you want to join and move in close to the circle – if someone notices you and moves to let you in step forward and acknowledge them – a quiet thank you, or at least a smile.

Here is a quote to remember from the Proverbs, "*Even a fool is thought wise if he keeps silent, and discerning if he holds his tongue.*" Restated by Abraham Lincoln, "*Better to remain silent and be thought a fool than to speak and to remove all doubt.*"

We are, after all, talking about *Motivational Listening.*

Your goal of attending the event is to connect with potential advocates, a group is not the best place for that; however, being in a group (and listening) will allow you to determine who might be a good advocate and someone you should follow up with.

Use Active Listening skills to track the flow of the conversation; don't try to just think about what you might say to break in.

Be interesting by being interested.

Note names and existing relationships of the group members. Do they know each other already; do they work together? Just as you would do your research on a famous person, listening to the discussion will provide you with your opportunity to connect with one of the members of this group.

If the members of this group are not discussing something that would be of interest, you can move on - there should be plenty of people at the event.

This is where you will need to be patient. Motivational Listening is intended to build rapport with an individual. The group setting is fine, if you are able to have a one-to-one conversation with a person while the others observe. It will work, because you are guiding the conversation and not the primary speaker. You are helping the speaker tell their story – and it is likely to be of interest to the other members of the group. In that group, focus on one person that will be the speaker and use the Motivational Listening process.

We continue the process in your verbal introduction.

Verbal Introduction:

After you've "tested the waters" and engaged with a new person (by engaging, I mean you have already now shared a few words). This is a part of the natural flow, and I want you to take the lead. When you were "testing the waters", you did not introduce yourself or offer contact information. You were determining if that person was interested in a conversation by using non-personal, non-threatening, and positive statements.

As we move to the next step in Motivational Listening at networking events, there are things to do and things to not do at this point.

Tell them your first name. if you are comfortable with providing your full name, then offer that. Some names are more challenging to understand in a crowded room. I do not have much problem with my name. Scott Smith is rarely mis-spelled or mis-pronounced. I lead with my full name.

“I’m Scott Smith” or just with my first name, “Hi, I’m Scott”

You have had a little chat with the speaker and you introduce yourself – almost ironically - like trading names is a little out of order. “Oh, by the way, I’m Scott”. If they do not respond by giving you their name, you have to ask, don’t let this moment pass. You absolutely must *remember their name*. Repeat it back to them at that moment.

“Terry, it’s great to meet you”

You can repeat something from your conversation they said (this is wonderful validation). “Pat, you are right about the speaker today.”

Things to not do:

Do not launch into your "elevator speech" or tag-line or anything beyond your name. You are working to be interesting by being interested. Motivational Listening, at its core, is for the speaker to exit the conversation feeling better about themselves than when they entered.

We want to keep the conversation away from us and focused on them.

You have enjoyed light conversation about the venue, food, or speaker, which is something that (at that moment) you have in common with that person. For the rest of existence the two of you will always have this event in common. You may not share any other interests or ever do business together, but today, you have this networking event in common which gives you an entry point to build rapport with them.

An important part of your connection with them: Remember their name. Do not forget their name. Name tags are helpful, but you cannot rely on them. Use the speaker's name right away. I am repeating this because it is critically important.

The Handshake:

At the same time that you are giving your verbal introduction, you extend your hand for a handshake. It is important that you say your name as you reach out your hand so they offer their name during the handshake.

We talked about the brain and the chemicals that are produced which impact our emotions and aid in connecting to others. One of the ways to release Oxytocin ("the trust molecule") is when we have physical contact. So, we shake hands. It is a culturally appropriate way of physical contact with a person we do not really know.

A good handshake: Look the person in the eye or at least in the face, just below and between the eyes is good, if not right into their eyeballs.

When you reach out, the position of your hand is subtly important. This is a meeting of equals. If you put your hand out with the palm down, that is demonstrating a dominant position; with the palm upward, that is a submissive position. Your hand should be perpendicular to the Earth. It is not pointing down to the ground or up to the sky; neither you nor the speaker are being forced to be either submissive or dominant, simply peers.

Have firm but not overpowering grip. Give their hand a couple of up and down movements and repeat their name after they tell it to you. The handshake should last about 2-3 seconds, but could go a bit longer if you need to have them repeat their name.

Opening Question:

You have "tested the waters", made name introductions, and stimulated the "trust molecule" with a handshake. Now it is time for your opening question. Remember people are daydreaming one-third to one-half of their waking hours; even though you think you have the speaker's attention you need to ensure you activate their Cognitive Functions by stimulating their Orbito-frontal Cortex.

The OFC portion of our brain responsible for face and voice recognition and is activated through error detection. When the unexpected happens, our OFC is activated and focuses our attention; a person can only focus on you if you lead with an unexpected question.

At networking events, there are a series of "expected" questions which are asked:

"How are you?"

"Enjoying the event?"

"What do you do?"

This type of question can be answered without thought. The speaker can still be thinking about where the car is parked, their schedule for tomorrow, or a myriad of items not connected with the answer they provide. It is a dead end question.

You need to be a little unexpected, not "over-the-top", and have something that fits within your personality. The question I open with will cause the speaker to pause, consider the question, and focus. The phraseology of the question I ask will vary, yet the fundamental is unchanged. I will ask:

"How's your world?"

"What's going on in your world?"

This question is not personal, I am not asking about them personally, rather about their environment. The nature of my question requires interpretation on their part. I can see the person's brain activate when I ask the question...they look up in the air as they consider, "what IS my world". They might interpret the question in terms of work, family, hobbies, or the event itself. You get interesting responses when you give people an opportunity to interpret your question.

You should develop your own opening question, and I give you full permission to use mine...find out what is going on in someone's world. I challenge you to ask this question the next time you are with the clerk at the checkout register. They will ask you expected questions, "how is your day", "did you find everything", and so forth. Answer them, then ask, "How is your world?" I am interested in the results when other share their experiences about asking this question.

The important part is that you are genuinely interested in learning about this person and that you want to build rapport.

Keep the question away from something personal – how they feel or what they think. We want to understand their environment; what is going on in their workplace, home life, and hobbies. You want to keep the question open to their interpretation, and let them set the direction for the content of your discussion to follow, one which you will guide.

Just a quick aside: You are at a networking event you want to build rapport with one person at a time. When you follow the Motivational Listening process, you will not have time (or energy) to talk to a lot of people. You will build connections with potential advocates. And as you have this conversation, you are striving to be interesting by being interested. You add to the conversation, while not simply setting up an opportunity to talk about yourself. Sharing bits about your life or experience is good, because you are not interrogating the speaker. You can let them know you share something in common with them or what they do is novel to you. Just keep the emphasis on them.

With your opening question, you have given them the opportunity to share a glimpse into the context of their life. You are now ready to take them on a conversational journey of their life to this point and remind them they have worked hard to be where they are, and that they are Remarkable.

Motivational Listener Step 2 – A Conversational Journey

As you guide the speaker on a conversational journey, you are going to ask about their personal history. You want to find out about their education and training (you want to understand their passion and motivation). This conversation will help you reveal what is in their Basal Ganglia – all this wonderful information and knowledge that, to them, seems like second nature or that it is simply common knowledge.

Personal History: Once you have a context for their life; whether it is work, home, hobby, or other, you can pursue the questions of discovery. This is a lot of fun. Most people may not realize this, but they probably have some pretty interesting life experiences, and you are going learn about the life of the speaker. Prepare to be amazed!

The next question you are going to ask will allow you to clarify, focus and lead into questions about their personal experience timeline. In response to your this question they may mention an occupation, their role in an organization, a geographic location, relationship, or other item of context, verify and validate what you heard.

"Ah, so you're a CPA"

"Your son just got married! Congratulations"

"You are new to the area"

There are many responses you will get, and they are all part of the context of the speaker's life. You will give a brief statement to let them know you have listened to what they were saying. And here you rely on your emotional intelligence based on their response to your summary – if you got it wrong, let them correct you and repeat the validation.

When they acknowledge that you correctly understand their context, quickly move to the next question. This conversation is about them; their natural and polite response at this moment is to ask about you. "What do you do" or something like that. If possible, ask your next question before they ask you. However, if they do ask you briefly state your function and quickly move right to a question for them.

Past, Present, and Future: We are with them in the present, we asked them about the context of their environment, now we are going into their past. They have just mentioned they are an accountant, teacher, business owner, and you verified your understanding. Now, ask them how long they have been in that role.

At this point we are taking them on a journey back from where they are to where they started. Where ever someone is today, they were someplace before that...no matter how long ago. They may be brand new to the area or job, or have some long-term tenure in what they do. Each of these is an opportunity to learn more. If they tell you they started with the company four months ago, your next question could be,

"What were you doing five months ago?" For the person that has been in the same career for 30+ years, you have an opportunity to learn how they chose to enter the field and what has kept their attention for such a long time. If the person has been several years with the same company, you can ask how they got started and what different roles they have had with the organization (it is not likely they are in the same job they started with). Perhaps they have been many years in the same job or location - you can ask them about the changes they have seen.

As you receive answers to your questions, more opportunities to ask them about the path they have taken will open. You will learn about the jobs they've taken, the education they received (sometimes it is not a formal school, but the school of life, or trial and error).

Our intention with this series of questions is to allow them to remember the journey of their life, the series of steps and choices they have taken (some of their choices may not have been so voluntary). We all get so busy with the tasks of our jobs and lives that it is all too easy to forget how hard we worked to arrive at our current point. Much of what we have learned has moved to the Basal Ganglia – it seems routine.

In just a few minutes, you have learned a great deal about this person. It is now time to summarize what you have learned, and recap the journey from where they were to where they are. Because you have a genuine interest in their life, and are allowing them to share their path, you will appear quite interesting. Now we have arrived to the time where you get to talk.

Motivational Listener Step 3 – Use Emotional Intelligence

Much of the process of Motivational Listening to this point could be described as almost "mechanical". The verbal greetings, handshakes, and questions can be programmed. The processes covered in this chapter and the next are not as simple. It will take practice (a bit of trial and error).

Earlier in the book I presented the complex topics of Emotional Intelligence and clues we can gather from micro-expressions. The Motivational Listener needs to use Emotional Intelligence during the conversation. Those that are skilled in using Emotional Intelligence are not ruled by their emotions. They are aware of their emotions and those of others around them. As a Motivational Listener, you use your skills to regulate your emotions and influence those of the speaker.

There will be times when your enthusiasm at attending a networking event is waning. You just "don't feel up to it". However, the present opportunity to build your network of advocates is now and you do not have the option to bail. It is critical you are able discern your emotional condition and control it.

"Fake it 'til you make it"? Perhaps.

The research from Killgore noted that the functioning of the brains of those with low emotional intelligence mirrored brains suffering from sleep deprivation. We also know that the effect of sleep deprivation is similar to that of intoxication. This leads me to this conclusion: since you would not show up drunk to a networking event, be certain to arrive well rested.

Your preparation for the event should include a plan on the type of advocate you seek (it could be a meeting with a specific person). You need to also need to get some sleep. A friend of mine posted to Facebook a request to find an "aggressive" alarm clock. He received a handful of suggestions ranging from an old style wind-up clock with bells to a rooster in his room. My suggestion was to find a clock that would make him go to bed 7-8 hours before he needed to rise. When your brain is not rested, your ability to control your emotions and recognize those of others is diminished. The emotional portions of your brain (e.g. amygdala responsible for the "flight or fight" response) will be more controllable when you have had enough sleep.

Engaging at networking events takes energy. Your network of advocates will grow when you are the one in control of the conversation and following the process of being a Motivational Listener.

Motivational Listener Step 4 – Differentiate Result and Motivation

At the end of the chapter on the Conversational Journey I mentioned it was finally your time to talk (and not only ask questions). I also added a chapter on Emotional Intelligence before we get to the part where you get to speak. Here is yet another chapter before you start talking because it's time to determine what you will be saying. It is all about them, and is based on what you have heard, observed, and extrapolated.

You have learned a lot about the speaker. What they do, how long they have been at it, what they were doing before what they are doing now, they may have told you about their background and education or information about their family.

All of this is a Result. Your task is to divine and understand the reason they do what they do, you want to discover their Motivation; what is it that has led them on this journey.

Of course, I'm not saying this is simple – it will take practice on your part.

There are a few points you will find as a trend, and be able to apply them in the various conversations you have at networking events. People care about something; they want to make a lasting impact (no one wants to be irrelevant). This is your golden moment to be truly interesting because you have been interested in their life.

Some common themes you will see are:

1 - Family or friends

2 - Health and security

3 - Quality of life (e.g. nutrition and exercise)

4 - Access to Education

From what you learned about the speaker, you will start to gain an understanding of their Motivation.

Let us look at a set of information (result) and make a determination as to the motivation: Should you observe me taking out a loaf of bread, jars of peanut butter and jelly – you are seeing the result of my motivation. It is quite simple. Instantly you know I am hungry (my motivation) and I am making a PB and J sandwich.

Nobody is going to see me with the sandwich ingredients and say, "Hey Scott is a sandwich man! He loves making sandwiches." We arrive at the conclusion that Scott is hungry. We are able to determine Motivation by observing the Result.

Speakers will tell us Results. If they tell us they are an accountant, attorney, or mechanic, each is the result of some specific motivation. I had a conversation with a person who owned a business that frames pictures. She got into the business because she loves art and is an artist. Result and Motivation.

Another person is working to be an attorney because she hates injustice. I have a friend who is a counselor because he understands the powerful benefits of strong families and marriages. Result and Motivation.

When you listen to the journey of the speaker and extract the Motivation from Result, you will be memorable, and they will see you as interesting.

Now it is your time to talk.

Motivational Listener Step 5 – Summarize and Remind Them They Are Remarkable

I have mentioned before that you must be genuine and authentic as a Motivational Listener. We are now coming to the end of the process and it will be apparent to the speaker if you are anything but truly interested.

In the 1993 movie, Ground Hog Day, Bill Murray's character experiences the same day repeatedly, reliving each event. He meets the same people, eats the same food, has the same conversations; and he remembers each of the previous days. In one segment of the movie they show him engaging in these conversations with no enthusiasm or passion, and certainly no interest. It is obvious to the other characters and to us in the audience that he is completely disengaged. We find the humor because he is simply "going-through-the-motions" of engaging with these people and it is painful to watch.

Do not be like Bill.

It is your time to talk, but it is not time to talk about yourself. You are going to:

1 - Present a summary of what you have heard

2 - Remind them of the journey they have taken

3 - Focus on their Motivation rather than on the Result

Let me jump right to some sample Result/Motivation combinations. I state a Result and a potential comment you can make to note the Motivation:

Accountant

Result: I am a CPA working with small business owners for payroll and tax work.

Motivation: I bet many businesses owners can sleep at night because they do not have to worry about a visit from the IRS because they work with you.

Teacher

Result: I am a third grade teacher

Motivation: Thank you for protecting our future by being a solid example and educating our children.

Mechanic

Result: I own an auto maintenance shop, working mainly with late model Japanese imports.

Motivation: I have looked under the hood of my car, and it is nothing like what I grew up with in my parent's garage. It must take a lot to keep up with the changes in today's cars. And you must feel good knowing your customers are safe while on the road.

Landscape contactor

Result: I am a landscaper. We design, install, and maintain yards, primarily for personal residences.

Motivation: There have probably been many beautiful selfies posted on Facebook in the yards you have designed and maintained. Lots of family memories captured in such wondrous surroundings.

What you heard was the Result (Accountant, Teacher, Mechanic, Landscape Contractor); what you shared back is their Motivation:

1 - Peace of mind

2 - Protecting the future

3 - Safety and security

4 - Family bonds and memories

You are reinforcing that the speaker's work has substance and meaning. It is an important step in the process of Motivational Listening because they may not realize the positive impact they have, and they may even feel as if what they do is irrelevant.

Early in this book I mentioned that our greatest fear is not pain or loss, but irrelevance. In just a few minutes, you have learned about this person and the results of their motivation. By restating what you learned about them in terms of the "good" they do, they feel better about themselves (a goal of Motivational Listening).

People are going to tell you "What" they do, and you are going to be a mirror that reflects the Motivation, the reason they have gone through all the effort to become an expert in their chosen field. They (and their families) have made sacrifices, paid hard dollars, and experienced a lot of trial and error (maybe a lot of error) to arrive where they are.

When you reflect back their Motivation, you are touching them in a part of their brain deeper than where we have language. The connection with you will be based on positive emotion. You use Emotional Intelligence to monitor the conversation to ensure you are on track. Your summary and connection between the result and motivation will not be long; a paragraph or two. The examples above are very quick. You don't have to talk long, just enough to summarize what you learned and giving it to them as a glimpse into their Motivation.

In applying your skills as a Motivational Listener at this networking event with a person you have never met before, you have built rapport, and developed a relationship with a potential advocate. You are ready for the last formal part of the process.

Motivational Listener Step 6 – Ask for Contact Information and Permission to Follow Up

The time available at a networking event is quite limited, and in some cases, quite structured. There might be a program or speaker or other activities, and the event has a beginning and end time. Before and after the event, you only have an empty room. The opportunity to build a network of advocates at that meeting is limited.

I recommend you do not waste time talking about yourself. Of course you are every bit as Remarkable. They can find out all about you and your company, products and services in a personal meeting after the event. When you schedule time to meet with them, you know enough to properly prepare; you can tailor your message to what is best for them. If you were to take networking time to talk about yourself (other than at a very high level) you are really only prepared to give generic responses.

Scheduled meetings have more impact than any impromptu meeting. If it is in someone's calendar it is documented and real. When your advocates talk about you in their network, the type of experience they have with you is important. When they do not yet know enough about you to be an advocate, they likely will not put their reputation on the line. A short conversation with you at an event is not enough for them to "know, like, and trust" you. If the only contact is at the networking event, they will not be telling people in their network how wonderful you are or the good work you do.

Get on their calendar. You will know based on your conversation if they have the potential to be a good advocate, and thereby if it is worth allocating time in your schedule to meet with them; it could be a simple phone call. It would be in your best interest to prepare, meet with them, and give them solid reasons to be your advocate. The goal is to put them into a position of knowledge about you so the referral to a friend or colleague starts with, "I had a meeting with someone who can help solve your problem." A much stronger introduction.

Now ask for their contact information. You can say, "It has been great chatting with you, learning how you help your clients. I would like to follow up with you and share information, perhaps grab a cup of coffee, do you have a card?" When you have their contact details, you can initiate the follow up. If you simply give them your card and you do not have their information, you are at the mercy of their time and follow-up skills.

I generally take five or fewer cards with me (unless it's a really large and long event or I am a speaker). My goal is to grow my network not hand out small pieces of paper. I have a friend that is in the printing business and during her entire career she has never had a printed business card. She always gets a card from potential advocates; she KNOWS there will be follow-up because she is in control and will reach out. At the follow up meeting I give them several of my cards so they can give them to those they would like to refer. That is a good use for business cards.

You combine the request for their contact information with a promise to follow up. If, during the conversation, you determine there is no need to follow up with them, do not ask for their card. The way you follow up could be a LinkedIn request, an email, phone call, or face-to-face meeting. I leave that to you.

You have done it! You cultivated a relationship with a potential advocate from a person you had never met. You accomplished this in just few minutes using the process of being a Motivational Listener.

Get their contact information and move along to other potential advocates at the networking event. You should capitalize on the people attending and find another person to connect with, repeating the Motivational Listening process.

Sometimes you need to disengage from a conversation. Excuse yourself; tell them you need to get a little more water, or that they might have other folks they need to talk with, or something that allows you to move into a conversation with another potential advocate. Always be polite.

It is helpful to note that this process of Motivational Listening is hard. It takes a lot of energy (working in your Prefontal Cortex, burning off a lot of glucose). It will be tiring, especially if you are an introvert. I also want to warn the extroverts to stay with the process and focus on one person at a time.

You have to pay attention and be nice. It is hard getting to know these folks. Remember, if it was easy, no one would do it. You are here for the challenge. Growing a business, your practice, or your network is hard work. And of course - you love it!

Final Summary of Networking Events

You are well on your way to building a network of advocates. I have given you a defined process to meet brand new people at networking events and quickly build rapport with them.

Let me summarize the steps of Motivational Listening. The formal steps you take after you have "Tested the Waters"

1 - Trigger their Cognitive Functions

Activate their Orbito-frontal cortex and stimulate the production of Oxytocin with a good handshake, verbal introduction, and a non-cliché opening question;

2 - Guide them on a conversational journey through their personal history

Find out about other occupations they have had after they tell you their current role, their education and training and where in the world they have been

3 - Summarize and let them know they are Remarkable

4 - Use Emotional Intelligence

5 - Differentiate between Result and Motivation

Result is what they tell you about themselves

Motivation is the reason they do what they do.

The speaker, in talking to you, will be explicit with what they do (the Result); a Motivational Listener will extract the latent motivation that drives their action.

6 - Close with a request for their contact information and permission to follow up

Congratulations on becoming a Motivational Listener! You've mastered the art of engaging others in a meaningful way, transforming an ordinary conversation into a fascinating journey.

You have learned to trigger cognitive functions, stimulating the orbito-frontal cortex and oxytocin production with a firm handshake, an articulate introduction, and intriguing non-cliché opening questions. You have found the knack of guiding your conversation partners through a journey of their personal history, probing into their past roles, education, training, and their global adventures.

As a Motivational Listener, you also possess the ability to make others feel remarkable by summarizing their story and acknowledging their uniqueness. Your emotional intelligence has blossomed, allowing you to navigate conversations with sensitivity and depth.

You have come to understand the crucial difference between results and motivations. While your conversation partner may openly share the results of their life - their roles, achievements, and experiences, you as a Motivational Listener, delve deeper. You extract the underlying motivations that drive their actions, shedding light on their deepest aspirations.

Finally, you have learned to wrap up your conversations tactfully, seeking contact information and gaining permission to follow up, ensuring your interaction doesn't end with just one conversation.

So, gear up for your next networking event with confidence. You're not just an ordinary participant anymore. You are a Motivational Listener - a person who is not just interesting, but genuinely interested in others. This powerful transformation promises enriching experiences, deeper connections, and a rewarding networking journey ahead.

Motivational Listener Cheatsheet

Motivational Listening is a defined process to connect with potential advocates that does not require you to be an extrovert nor is it limited by being an introvert. There are six steps to use Motivational Listening at networking events:

1. ACTIVATE COGNITIVE FUNCTIONS

Research tells us we daydream between 30%-50% of our waking hours. This is true when you are connecting at a networking event. Your potential advocate can be thinking about the food, where they parked, or any number of things when you approach them. There is a portion of the brain that activates when the unexpected happens. The Orbito-frontal cortex focuses attention and snaps a wandering mind away from daydreams. You activate this cognitive function with an unexpected question. I like to ask, "How's your world?" It is non-threatening and not too strange.

2. TAKE THEM ON A CONVERSATIONAL JOURNEY

Your goal is to get to know this person by asking questions, it is not your time to blurt your elevator speech or tagline. Get to know them – what they do, how they got interested in this career, and what has changed. This allows you to become interesting by being interested.

3. REMIND THEM THEY ARE REMARKABLE

Once you have learned about the speaker's career journey, compliment them on the effort it took and how they are solving problems for people. People often forget how much they know because the knowledge becomes "hard wired" into their brain through a process called Neuroplasticity. Use this opportunity to remind them that what they do is remarkable.

4. USE EMOTIONAL INTELLIGENCE

The ability to control your emotions and influence the emotions of others is Emotional Intelligence. It is important to control your emotions when attending networking events. Sometimes the conversations might include a topic where you have a strong emotion. Remember, this is not a debate. A networking event is to connect with advocates not to prove a point.

5. DIFFERENTIATE RESULT AND MOTIVATION

The answers you receive from the speaker during the conversational journey will provide you Results. If you ask a person's profession and they tell you they are an accountant (result) it might be because they value the beauty of order in numbers (motivation); an engineer (result) may be motivated by solving problems (motivation). If you can separate the speaker's motivation from the result, you will demonstrate a deeper understanding of their business, and thereby a deeper connection.

6. CLOSE FOR CONTACT DETAILS AND PERMISSION TO FOLLOW-UP

Once you have made a connection with a person at the networking event you can gracefully disengage by thanking them and asking for contact details. You do not want to dominate their time or limit your ability to meet other potential advocates. The follow-up meeting is the time to provide details about your business. The message you will share about your company at that meeting can be tailored to them based on what you have learned.

Relationships: Grow Your Business

So, gear up for your next networking event with confidence. You're not just an ordinary participant anymore. You are a Motivational Listener - a person who is not just interesting, but genuinely interested in others. This powerful transformation promises enriching experiences, deeper connections, and a rewarding networking journey ahead.

I was under a misunderstanding that you should never tell anyone what you do – give away the secrets – because they would never hire you. They go the “do-it-yourself” route and you’d lose a sale. Then I was watching a Penn and Teller video on YouTube where they explain, step-by-step, how to perform the classic sleight of hand trick known as cups and balls.

Penn and Teller perform this remarkable trick with three cups and a number of balls. Then they went through every movement, very slowly, so you could follow along at home. Still, I couldn’t perform this trick. They went one step further with the demonstration by replacing the standard cups with clear cups. Now I could see what was happening as they went through each step.

I still can't perform the cups and balls trick. They are masters at what they do. If I was going to host a birthday party (and could afford them) I'd hire Penn and Teller. That would not be the time for a DIY solution.

It's the same in all our businesses. We have expertise. Those who will go the DIY route will do so regardless of how mysterious you are about your process. Let people know what you do, and the ones you can help will come your way.

The reality is: people are not interested in what you do. They want results. They want to know the outcome of working with you. No one wants to spend money on the wrong solution. Let them know the outcome and how you help them get the results they seek. This is part of the "content marketing" strategy. Keep giving value so they trust you enough to spend real money.

My Promise (outcome) for This Section

Your social media feeds and email inbox is filled with promises of $10k months and 6-figure years. That's pretty enticing. Your business may be capable of those types of numbers. I won't make such a promise. What I can tell you: I am the sole income for my family, and I do this only on referrals. One hundred percent of my clients have come through relationships.

I mentioned those offers you see daily. They have a similar message. Now, I'm not implying what is offered is not worth the money – for the right business. You'll hear that to be successful you need to write a book, speak on stages, grow your Instagram following, run paid ads, or go viral on TikTok. If you do this one thing, you'll make money.

These might work. They all have the same formula: solve a significant problem (deliver an outcome) and let potential customers know what you have to offer. If you do this, you'll make money. Whether you have fabulous Instagram Reels, LinkedIn Live videos, or compelling content on Twitter Spaces – it's getting your message to the right people.

In this book I will give you my proven formula to grow your business without paid ads or mastering a social media platform. Your business may be capable of scaling to hundreds of clients – this may not be for you. I am speaking directly to the solo entrepreneur, freelance professionals, and small business owner that really only need a handful of clients, and that would be enough to support you and your family.

A repeatable and consistent system to get new clients means I don't have to follow the newest trend. I don't have to spend money on systems designed for big business. My network is filled with more potential clients than I can serve. This means I spend time not working and vacations are possible. If I want to take a weekend away, or spend the day hiking, it's not an issue. I know how I'll make my mortgage payment.

Your Takeaway

In this section of the book you will learn my proprietary system to analyze and leverage you professional network. You will have the tools to grow your business through your business relationships. It's not magic. It is work.

In the following chapters of this book, you'll get what you need to grow your business to any scale you desire. You might be ready and wanting those $10k months. Maybe not. Either way, you will have everything you need to succeed.

Why do we hate networking?

I think networking gets a bad rap. It's like people in sales are often equated with the plaid-jacketed, over-zealous used car salesman. We've had bad experiences at networking events. The notice we received said something like, "Come to our business after hours and get referrals!"

At least, that's the expectation we've been given. Join the Chamber of Commerce or your local BNI group and you'll have an active sales force sending referrals to you. I've been a member of these organizations – and they are good (for what they're good at). I was a board member of our local chamber for 9 years. I strongly support chambers of commerce and referral groups like BNI.

I used to be so frustrated after attending networking events. I thought I'd simply share what I do and folks would start "hooking me up". Now I understand why one of my clients (an engineer's engineer from the heart of Silicon Valley) told me, "Scott, as soon as walk into a networking event I wonder 'how long to I have to stay before it's rude of me to leave.'"

We feel like it's going to be 90 minutes of bad hors d'oeuvre and hard sells. People walking up to you, shaking your hand, and introducing themselves and asking what you do. But what they are really asking is, "how can I make money off you?"

Now that I've "set the stage" let's get into meat of the Motivational Listener Professional Network System.

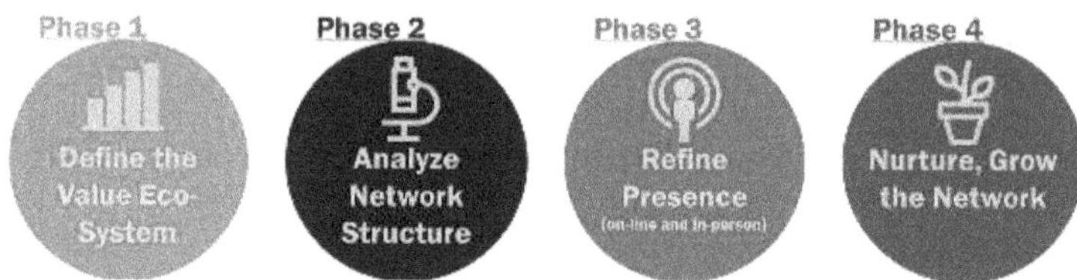

In my Motivational Listener Professional Network System there are four phases:

1 – Define the Value Ecosystem:

People are looking for solutions to problems. We define the value you offer. You have the right solution for the right customer; they need what you have to offer. Don't make them wait any longer.

2 – Analyze Your Network Structure:

Your professional network consists of those who have direct experience working with you; those with first-hand experience; and finally, those with credible experience of your work. We evaluate the network structure, identify gaps, and a path to build the perfect network.

3 – Refine Your Presence (on/offline):

Successfully achieving dreams, goals, and objectives will be supported by the perfect business network. It's not who you know. It's who knows you. We refine your presence to be known.

4 - Nurture and Grow Your Network:

Effective use of your professional network is not a one-time exercise; care must be taken to cultivate relationships. Intentional execution of your strategy will ensure long-term career and business success.

Phase 1: Define the Value-Eco System

Your Network

The great news: you already have a fabulous network filled with people wanting you to succeed. They simply need to know what problem you solve and who would be a good prospect. It's really not any more difficult than that.

There are three things you need for a business. It's not a website, clever business name, snappy tagline, or well-rehearsed "elevator pitch". The three things you need (and they must be present to have a business) are:

1 - Problem – this is the pain someone is experiencing, and they want to be rid of this issue

2 - Solution – this is what you have to offer. It ends the pain

3 - Customer – this is the person with the pain who has decided that the cost of your solution is less than living with the pain

We know potential clients have problems. They are not interested in your solution. They are interested in what life will be like when the problem is gone. They want an outcome. However, we often become enamored with our own solution – so that is what dominates our conversation.

Features and Benefits

In sales you may have heard of Features and Benefits. Features are the technical aspects of the solution, and Benefits are aspects that make it attractive to a potential customer. The common saying is, "Features tell. Benefits sell."

The one thing I can say about that, it rhymes.

We are missing the third column. There are features and benefits, however there is still something missing. The third column is "Who Cares".

NOTE: I apologize for the dorky name of this important aspect. I'd much rather have it flow better. Feature, Benefits, Who Cares is not so catchy, but it does cover the intent of this critical item.

Let's look at personal fitness because most of us can relate.

A health club has a facility designed to house fitness equipment and space. They also employ personal trainers who have been trained and certified. An individual can sign up for the health club and enroll with a personal trainer.

Now let's break down the Features, Benefits, and see where Who Cares fits into the sales mix.

Features (technical specifications) offered:

1 - Facility is open 24 hours each day

2 - Modern equipment is maintained and updated regularly

3 - All trainers have appropriate certifications

4 - Personal fitness plans are created for individuals enrolled with trainers

These seem fine and standard. Not compelling me to buy. Let's look at the Benefits because we've been told, "Benefits sell."

Benefits (make it attractive) based on the features:

1 - Convenient – you never have to wonder if the club is open 24/7

2 - You'll always have the best equipment clean and in working order

3 - Whether your goal is cardio vascular, flexibility, or general health, the right certified trainer will help you meet your needs and goals

4 - Your personal trainer will keep you accountable. You won't be trying to reach your goals on your own. Your trainer will ensure you are doing the right exercises, on schedule, to meet your goals

These types of benefits are often what we hear in the marketing message. The ad may refer to the Features, but the message will emphasize the Benefits (because they sell, right?).

Let's add the third column. This is where niching down is important. Not everyone is experiencing the same problem; but many groups of people do have similar needs. Here's what we might find in the third column:

Who Cares (why is this important to me) and if most often missing:

1 - A 55 year old grandfather is watching his grandchild play on the soccer field

2 - The child asks, "Grandpa, will you play with me?"

3 - Are you the grandpa that tires in just a few minutes of kicking the ball around?

4 - Or, are does your grandchild ask, "Grandpa, can we rest for a bit?"

This is the power of Who Cares. It must be a specific message to a specific audience. They know you understand the problem and what Outcome they desire. That grandfather is not paying attention to the Features or Benefits, they heard you say they will be able to enjoy the grandkids.

That sells.

Share Your "Who Cares" with Your Network

Examine what problem you solve, who is your ideal customer, and be prepared to clearly state the "Who Cares" aspect of your offer. This is what you will present to your network. In doing this simple exercise, those in your network are now ready to let the right people know about you and your solution.

If you are a marker, people don't care about email sequences, funnels, or being top in Google searches. Those are simply substitutes for their Who Cares, for the outcome and results. In the example of the health club, it was spending quality time with grandkids. Find the Who Cares and share this with those in your network.

This brings us to Phase 2: Analyzing the Network Structure. Not everyone in your network will send referrals your way. There are defined roles within your network. In the next chapter we will examine what those are and provide tools to examine your network.

NOTE: What's the outcome of reading this section of the book?

You may have read it earlier:

"A repeatable and consistent system to get new clients means I don't have to follow the newest trend. I don't have to spend money on systems designed for big business. My network is filled with more potential clients than I can serve. This means I spend time not working and vacations are possible. If I want to take a weekend away, or spend the day hiking, it's not an issue. I know how I'll make my mortgage payment."

Phase 2: Analyze Your Network Structure (this is proprietary material)

You won't find this in any material by Zig Ziglar or Tony Robbins, or other business experts. The only place to find what I will tell you is in the Motivational Listener Professional Network System. I have codified what was working for me and others who are successful at getting customers from their professional networks.

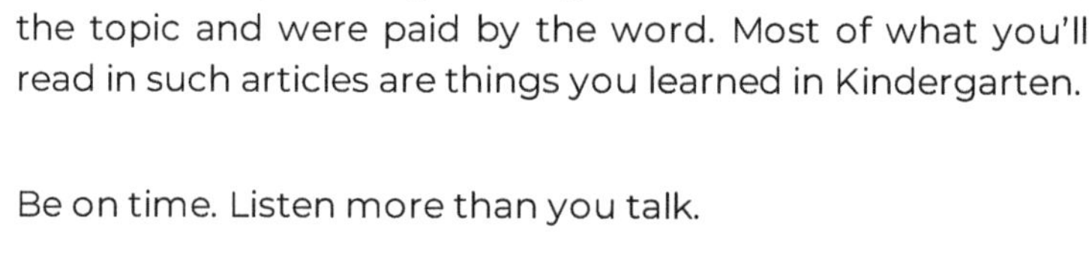

I have read many articles on business networking. Most of these were topics assigned to good writers who researched the topic and were paid by the word. Most of what you'll read in such articles are things you learned in Kindergarten.

Be on time. Listen more than you talk.

Don't go right for the sale.

Build relationships first.

Use good body language.

Be an active listener.

Follow through on commitments.

While these are all true, they are the fundamentals of politeness, but not a system or method to build a professional network.

I mentioned in the first section of this book, "Your network is your net worth". When we consider our business network, we think we either have to learn to play golf, attend mind-numbing mixers, or join the local chamber of commerce.

There is nothing magical about golf course. It is simply people with a common interest spending time together. The result: a relationship is built. It is natural to do business together. They know, like, and trust each other.

Networking is simply the process of intentionally building relationships.

Components of Your Professional Network

A professional network is effective when we connect with the right people and offer the right solutions. We build relationships when we connect with people, those meetings can occur on a golf course, business mixer, trade show, or chamber event. We can connect in-person or virtually. The manner depends on your preferences and business need.

Building an effective business network consists of more than attending events; networking events are simply one method of meeting the right people. In this phase I introduce you to the structure of your professional network.

Extended and Active Networks

Extended Networks

Networks are interconnected nodes. Our business networks are enormous. The average person on LinkedIn has 1,500 connections. How often have you looked at someone's profile on LinkedIn and notice they are a second-level connection, that is, you share a contact but are not yet connected to each other.

I have a modest number of connections on LinkedIn – now approaching 2,700. I guarantee that I do not know 2,700 people. But this aspect of my business network is important. I do not know 2,700 people but these people comprise my Extended Network.

My Extended network is important because this extends my reach. As my buddy Ted Rubin says, "Networks give you reach. Relationships give you power."

Our Extended Network can consist of thousands of individuals. LinkedIn is the business standard (currently) for business connection; this is why I like to use this to explain the Extended Network. This large network gives me good reach, but it's not where the power is found. Many of the people in my Extended Network are one-time connections. We sat together at lunch during a tradeshow or had a conversation at a networking event.

It's not who you know. It's who knows you. Many of those in my Extended Network do not know me and would not answer my phone call or open my email. The power found in our Active Network.

Active Network

I've found that when we use a critical eye on our Extended Network and reduce it to those with whom we'd actually conduct business or send referrals, the number is around 100-150 persons. This agrees with the work of British anthropologist, Robin Dunbar.

In the 1990s Dunbar proposed that we are capable of maintaining around 150 stable relationships. Our individual capacities will differ; the 150 number is an average. When we examine our Extended Network and assign one of five defined roles, we generally arrive at between 100 and 150 people in the Active Network.

Your Active Network will have these five distinct roles:

1 - Advisors and Mentors

2 - Mentees

3 - Customers (or employers)

4 - Advocates

5 - Partners

Advisors and Mentors

This group may only be around 3% of your total Active Network. These are the people you turn to when making business or life decisions. Your trusted advisors offer guidance and advice. You may meet with them on a regular schedule or "as needed".

Mentees

Mentees will be the smallest group in you Active Network and may only be one or two people. There are a number of reasons you should have Mentees. First – it's the right thing to do. We should be adding our experiences and knowledge into the next generation. Second – the teacher always learns more than the teacher. When you have to encode and transmit your information to another person, you formulate it in a way that makes sense. In doing this, it often clarifies the details in your own brain.

Customers (or employers)

Customers could be a quarter of your Active Network. Customers are a good source of repeat business and they have direct experience working with you and therefore can be a referral source. Current customers are definitely in your Active Network; past customers may be if you are maintaining contact.

Advocates

Advocates are those individuals willing to publically promote you and your work. These are where you will receive the bulk of your referrals. However, this is not a large group; Advocates may only be 8-12% of your total Active Network.

Partners

This is the largest group in your Active Network. Partners are those who solve problems you don't but allow you to add value to your network. I often refer to this group as the "who's you plumber?" You may ask me if I know of a good plumber, and I will tell you someone I trust from my Partners. I become an Advocate for the plumber. I would not expect the plumber to refer customers to me. That is not the role of a Partner in my Active Network. However, because I was able to connect you to a solution to your problem, my value in the network increases.

Relative Active Network Structure

Your Active Network is unique to you. There are relative percentages of each role within your network. The chart below provides an approximation of a healthy Active Network structure.

Active Network Distribution

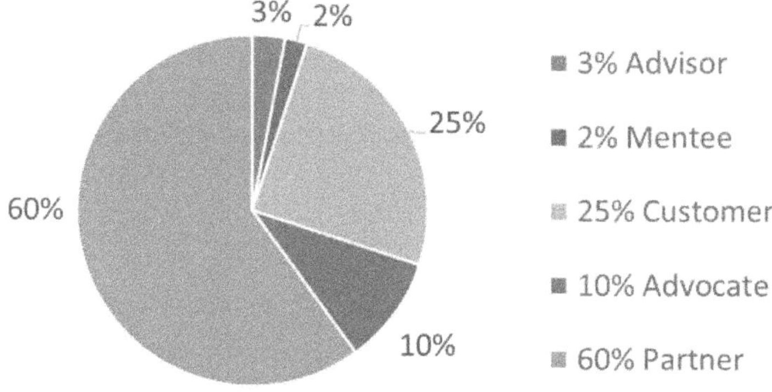

Phase 3: Refine Your Online and In-Person Presence

Mindset

We know that mindset is an important aspect of your in-person and online presence. In this phase we look at the components of your presence and message for face-to-face or digital presentation. We will not be crafting an "elevator pitch". (I find the elevator pitch to be on the same plane as autoresponders and impersonal.)

The presence you create and project are based on your self-view. In our culture, we do not place braggarts in high regard. We may consider them to be arrogant. Knowing you solve a problem and you letting others know you solve this problem is not being arrogant.

There are two types of people that demonstrate full competence: arrogant and confident. Both are capable of successfully solving the problem. However, the arrogant person takes while the confident person gives. You can let others know what you do in full confidence.

Research tells us attractive people are more successful. Further research also tells us that confident people are more attractive. Referring to high school algebra: if A = B; and, B = C; then, A = C. Confident people are more successful (using the Transitive Property from mathematics).

Having a confident mindset is important in growing your business and being successful.

Online Presence

Our online presence may be the first thing potential connections in our network see. Let's focus, again, on LinkedIn. Does your photo represent you well? We should have a professional quality headshot taken every couple of years. Head, shoulders, looking at the camera, and smiling.

I've some of the worst photos on LinkedIn profiles. Selfies in the car, or cropping another person out of the shot. None of these lend an air of professionalism. Keep it simple and smile.

I've now mentioned "smile" twice in the same number of paragraphs. The human brain is wired to see the human face. When we see someone smiling, it's natural for us to mirror. Psychologists have found that by simply smiling we will feel happier. In a 2019 paper from the University of Texas at Knoxville, we read that the facial expressions of others can affect our feelings. So, smile!

Under photo is your name. Use upper and lower case. This may seem rudimentary, but I see so many people using all lower case – it feels diminutive. If you have a designation (CPA, MBA, PhD, etc.) add that as well.

Now you get to add a line of description. In most cases on LinkedIn, I find people treating this like a corporate business card. In that rat race (am I showing my bias?), titles are something to be sought, earned, and respected.

I see so many people using the description line to tout their title: Senior Vice President, Managing Director, Executive Director, and the most common CEO or Chief Executive Officer.

When I was a part of a small startup and making the pitch circuits, everyone was "CEO and Founder". I remember raising more than a few eyebrows when I stepped up to the mic and said, "It's kind of funny to stand here and tell you I'm the CEO when my entire company could have come here in the same mini-van."

They were somewhat appeased when I said that my title of CEO made my mother happy.

Do not waste this real estate my using your title. Back when I was in banking, my father told me (trying to dislodge me from the profession) that, "In banking everyone's a vice president and nobody makes any money." Put your tilted on your card and send one to your mother.

In the description you want to describe what problem you solve, who has the problem, and (if possible) the time frame. The best one I've seen recently said, "I help successful business owners start and launch their podcast in 60 days or less."

BOOM!

One last "pet peeve" I will share with you. If you are a business, dump the Gmail email. When I see a professional with an xxxxx@gmail.com address, I am disappointed. If you are a real business, get a domain and business email. It's not hard and it's not expensive.

In Person Presentation

In your conversations you need to have "talking points", snippets of your message that connect the client problem to your solution. I mentioned that I am not a fan of the "elevator pitch". This word-smithed, and well-rehearsed message is a supposed to have come from script writers tying to pitch movie ideas to producers by trapping them in an elevator and spewing their idea in the time it takes for the elevator to move between floors.

I don't recall ever hearing such a tactic working.

Earlier in this book I mentioned that you already have a wonderful network filled with remarkable people who want you to win. They simply need to know what problem you solve and who would be a good prospect.

Talking points are a much more versatile tool than the elevator pitch. Talking points allow you to tailor your message and present it in a relational manner.

Let me breakdown my networking coaching program into a set of talking points:

1 – Outcome:

Reliable/repeatable method to get referrals

Growing a business by leveraging business relationships

2 – Audience:

Solo entrepreneurs

Freelance professionals

Small business owners

Growing a business by "word-of-mouth" (referrals vs. paid advertising)

3 – Time frame:

30-90 days

4 - Process or method

4 Phase method

I now have defined the problem I solve; the group who can benefit; the time frame to achieve the outcome; an overview of my system to reach the outcome; and additional resources. I can address these in a manner that is appropriate for the person I am speaking with, either in person or online.

Phase 4: Nurture and Grow the Network

Extended & Active Networks

You have invested a significant amount of time to define the value ecosystem, analyze the network structure, and refine your online and in-person presence. You already have a fantastic network filled with remarkable people who want you to succeed.

Now that you can clearly articulate the problem you solve and ideal customer, it's time to nurture this network and strategically grow.

Now the long-term process begins to nurture and deepen existing relationships and fill gaps in your Active Network. If you already use a client management tool (CRM), then add tags to those who belong in our Active Network based on their specific role:

Advisor/Mentor
Mentee
Customer
Advocate
Partner

If you do not use a CRM, a spreadsheet and calendar work well.

Frequency of Contact

You may have heard you should reach out to a certain number of people each day to maintain or grow your professional network. While this is true, it is important to and to have a plan and process on who to contact. Random processes generate random results.

Here is the frequency I recommend:

Advisors/Mentors: **Weekly**
Mentees: **Weekly**
Customers: **Monthly**
Advocates: **Monthly**
Partners: **Annually**

When we consider when to contact members of your Active Network, I recommend sticking with traditional work days. The average month has 20 work days. Depending on the number of individuals in your Active Network, you will need to reach out to 3-5 people each day. Here are a couple of examples based on networks of 100 and 150:

	Active Network size	100		
Role	Percentage	Number	Frequency	Annual Calls
Advisor	3%	3	Weekly	150
Mentee	2%	2	Weekly	100
Customer	25%	25	Monthly	300
Advocate	10%	10	Monthly	120
Partner	60%	60	Annually	60
			Annual Calls	730
	© 2021 D. SCOTT SMITH CO.		Calls/day	3.0

The method of contact will be determined by your style and the preferences of the person in your network. You can make in-person visits, phone calls, text or DM, email, hand written notes, or any other number of methods. The key is daily consistency. This needs to move from intention, to habit, to routine.

In this book, I have presented practical tools and method about the dynamics of business networking. We examined the brain science of connection, shedding light on the neurological basis of how we form connections and relationships. This understanding provided a base for developing strategies that harness our inherent cognitive abilities to foster meaningful relationships.

I then presented my unique six-step process designed to maximize your effectiveness at networking events. This method, drawn from years of experience and refined through practical application, is crafted to not only facilitate new connections but also to deepen existing relationships. Its focus lies in transforming these often-overlooked opportunities into a valuable tool for personal and professional growth.

Building upon this, I introduced a proprietary structure for creating and maintaining a strong business network. This strategic framework allows for the sustainable development of your professional network, nurturing relationships that provide value, encourage growth, and open doors to new opportunities.

Throughout the book, I emphasized the compelling connection between confidence, success, and networking. Confident people are more successful. Walking into a networking event with a structure and plan significantly contributes to building confidence. A strong professional network does not only improve our professional lives; it positively impacts our overall well-being, leading to increased happiness, health, and longevity.

Business networking is the most effective and efficient form of marketing for small business owners and solo entrepreneurs. Through an understanding of the science of connection and applying practical strategies, we turn networking from a daunting task into an enriching experience.

Remember: You Are Remarkable!

About The Author:

D. Scott Smith is a collaborator sitting in the juncture of strategy and execution. He is known as a Motivational Listener. Scott is a mentor, advisor, and coach who will inspire and motivate you. His company works with businesses and individuals across the county and around the world.

Prior to becoming a full-on entrepreneur, Scott worked in large and small companies in leadership roles which include CEO, COO, and General Manager. He has lived and breathed financial services, agriculture, and manufacturing. Scott is involved with joint ventures because he believes in the power of networking. He speaks on Motivational Listening, Leadership, and Intentional Change.

Scott and his wife, Christine, are enjoying being "empty nesters". Three children, one dog, one cat, and an undisclosed number of fish inhabit their lives. Scott usually has a guitar handy and might be found at your local Blues Jam.

Contact Scott directly with inquiries for coaching, consulting, and speaking. Visit his website dscottsmith.com to learn more about becoming a Motivational Listener. Send him an email: scott@dscottsmith.com or find him on Twitter @d_scott and Instagram @d.scottsmith

It's not about making money.

It's about living a life that makes a difference.

www.ingramcontent.com/pod-product-compliance
Ingram Content Group UK Ltd.
Pitfield, Milton Keynes, MK11 3LW, UK
UKHW022020190726
13853UKWH00005B/2031

9 798869 254801